STOLEN MOMENTS

Stolen Moments

CONVERSATIONS WITH CONTEMPORARY MUSICIANS

Tom Schnabel

ACROBAT BOOKS • LOS ANGELES

780.92 S357s
Schnabel, Tom.
Stolen moments

COPYRIGHT © 1988 BY TOM SCHNABEL

NO PART OF THIS BOOK MAY BE REPRODUCED IN ANY FORM OR BY ANY ELECTRONIC OR MECHANICAL MEANS INCLUDING INFORMATION STORAGE AND RETRIEVAL SYSTEMS WITHOUT PERMISSION IN WRITING FROM THE PUBLISHER, EXCEPT BY A REVIEWER, WHO MAY QUOTE BRIEF PASSAGES IN A REVIEW.

PUBLISHED BY ACROBAT BOOKS, P.O. BOX 480820, LOS ANGELES, CA 90048

LIBRARY OF CONGRESS CATALOG CARD NUMBER: 88-071632

BOOK DESIGN BY P*h*.D.

FIRST PRINTING 1988

MANUFACTURED IN THE UNITED STATES OF AMERICA

I would like to dedicate this book to John Coltrane,
a constant source of inspiration,
and to the incredible talking drummers
in Chief Commander Ebeneezer Obey's band.

And, with love, to Peggy.

"WITHOUT MUSIC, LIFE WOULD BE A MISTAKE."
—*Friedrich Nietzsche*

CONTENTS

Foreword ix

Introduction xi

John Adams 3
King Sunny Ade 7
Mose Allison 11
Laurie Anderson 17
Joan Baez 23
Jonathan Borofsky 29
David Byrne 35
Johnny Clegg 41
Leonard Cohen 49
Michael Feinstein 55
Philip Glass 59
Joe Jackson 65
Keith Jarrett 71
Kiri Te Kanawa 79
Miriam Makeba 83

STOLEN MOMENTS

Branford Marsalis	91
John McLaughlin	97
Francis Paudras	101
Penguin Cafe Orchestra	111
Astor Piazzolla	117
Steve Reich	123
Robbie Robertson	129
Ryuichi Sakamoto	137
Ravi Shankar	143
Wayne Shorter	153
Nina Simone	159
Nicolas Slonimsky	163
Mercedes Sosa	175
Richard Stoltzman	179
Yma Sumac	185
Tangerine Dream	191
Bertrand Tavernier	195
Andreas Vollenweider	199
Tom Waits	205
Joe Zawinul	211
Discography	217

FOREWORD

VARIETY IS THE SPICE OF LIFE. WE ALL KNOW THAT. BUT TODAY, THERE is a new explosion of excitement as the combining of music from all cultures and languages accelerates. This book documents and bears witness to the emergence of a new sensibility.

It is like the dance of chromosomes as they divide and recombine, creating new hybrid life forms. What emerges will inevitably be the music and cultural forms of the 90's.

Of course. Why not!

STOLEN MOMENTS, and the radio program it is drawn from, *Morning Becomes Eclectic,* are examples of the power of mixing disparate elements. The show has been running for nine years, while many "commercial" radio formats have come and gone, demonstrating—to carry the genetic metaphor further—that there is strength in variety. Our love of music and culture need not be confined to one style.

This is a book of conversations with some of the people I have most admired, been most influenced by, and have most wanted to meet. Imagine, Tom Schnabel does this for a living! His work gives one hope and encouragement.

STOLEN MOMENTS

If the dissemination of western pop music and culture throughout the world threatens to create a mono-culture, then here is welcome evidence that it is not succeeding completely. Music is not a universal language, thank goodness. We do not hear a recording of a *kora* player from Senegal in the same way as the people there do. Even modern western "classical" music, or jazz, is both loved and hated by people within its own culture.

Our culturally biased assumptions may ultimately work in our favor, though, if they are tempered with compassion and tolerance for those whose world-view (and musical life) is different from our own. Every culture, including ours, filters what it receives through its own sensibility, and eventually reshapes its musicial environment to meet its own ends. Rhumbas played by Africans become something else. Indian modal systems interpreted by Afro-American jazz musicians are no longer recognizably Indian. New forms and hybrids are created, the best retaining some cultural identity while bringing forth something unique. The world is the richer for it, the gift has been passed on—in somewhat mutated form.

The people in this book might be considered reporters of another kind of news—the news that passes from heart to heart.

Oddly enough, one senses in these various conversations a single voice, or entity—one that has trouble speaking directly about music. It circles around the subject, seeing different aspects from different points of view but never the whole thing. One has to put all these pieces together in one's own head.

The consciousness that emerges touches us deeply through a total abstraction—music—and we still don't know how or why.

It often seems we live in a world bent on self-destruction and increasing uglification, and efforts to hold back this rising tide seem futile. But the existence of this singular book, and the music that inspires it, offers a ray of hope. Here is proof that all over the world a simple and subtle form of resistance is taking place.

If our lives are made whole through these moments of beauty and love, these glimpses of the mysterious and ineffable in all acts of creation—whether by nature, art, or labor—then here is food for the soul. What else have we got?

—DAVID BYRNE   JULY, 1988

INTRODUCTION

THIS BOOK CONTAINS THE BEST INTERVIEWS FROM HUNDREDS I'VE done over the past nine years on my weekday music program, *Morning Becomes Eclectic.* I am grateful to be able to do a music show that embraces so many types of music. Radio experts told us from the beginning that such a mixed format would never work. My experience has been quite the contrary. More than ever before I find there exists a public eager to hear music, both old and new, from all over the world.

    This book embodies my love of music, a passion that started in high school when I'd lock myself in my room, listening to John Coltrane records at full volume on an old Magnavox console, driving my parents and siblings crazy. It is about my fascination for the substance and spirit of music, this ethereal and invisible art form that can grab you so powerfully and make you laugh, dance or cry. I studied literature in college, but always felt a more immediate emotional connection with music: Language was often slippery, deceptive and, at worst, dishonest.

    I share this passion with the many people I spoke with in these pages. With one exception all these interviews were done live, usually without any prior meeting or contact with the artists except through their music. I thank each one of them for taking time out of busy schedules to talk with me, a complete stranger. I usually had less than an hour to establish a precious trust. Sometimes conversations flowed effortlessly, sometimes they were awkward and uneasy. This collection stands as a tribute to these artists and their work, and I hope you enjoy reading it as much as I've loved putting it together.

I would like to thank, first, KCRW's General Manager, Ruth Hirschman, for granting me permission to use material drawn from the many interviews I've done, and for supporting my musical vision from the beginning. I also wish to thank Peggy Fogelman, Maya Cohan, Sarah Spitz, John Schaefer, and Ara Guzelimian for poring over the rough drafts, giving me invaluable insights and suggestions. I also am grateful to my assistant in the music department of KCRW, Ariana Morgenstern, for helping arrange many of the interviews, and for her support in general. I also must thank the music staff of KCRW: I have learned a great deal about music from all of them. I also gratefully credit Masako Takahashi for helping arrange clearances for publication.

Finally, I thank my editor, Tony Cohan, for his tireless work and unflagging encouragement throughout this project. Without his supreme effort and inspiration, STOLEN MOMENTS would never have come about.

—TOM SCHNABEL   JULY, 1988

"My first piece was performed by the New Hampshire State Mental Hospital. Frequently these patients sort of went off the wall..."

JOHN ADAMS

WHILE RICHARD NIXON'S NAME SKULKS THROUGH THE HEADlines of our era, who would imagine him as the central figure of an opera? Perhaps it took a composer whose first publicly performed work was by the inmates of a mental hospital to bring us the sweeping, audacious, controversial opera, Nixon in China.

There is something very American about the music of John Adams; he will use the poems of Emily Dickenson, or attempt in his Shaker Loops to capture the frenzied ecstasy of the early American religious sect. In person he was both reserved and humorous, a lively, intelligent man to talk with.

TS: You were born back East, weren't you?

JA: In Worcester, Massachusetts, or as the natives call it, "Woostah." Actually my parents moved within a year or two of my birth to Vermont and lived in a very small town there. Then when I was about eight years old I moved to New Hampshire, which is an equally small state, in the heart of New England. I grew up there, then went back to Boston to college. So even though I've been living in California now for almost seventeen years, I still feel like a Yankee. I don't think I'll ever quite feel like a surfer.

TS: Were you always interested in music?

JA: Yeah. Both of my parents were musicians, neither of them professionals. But my mother was a jazz singer and my father played saxophone and clarinet. They met at the dance hall that my mother's stepfather owned. It was called, "Irwin's Winnipesaukee Gardens," a beautiful old dance hall built on pilings over Lake Winnipesaukee in central New Hampshire. I think it was about 1936 or so. My dad played in a swing band. They met there one summer and eloped.

TS: When did you decide to become a composer?

JA: That's hard to say. I think it's kind of strange that a kid six or seven years old would have fantasies of being a composer, of writing music. I did. Maybe that's just an indication of the aberration of the field. I think I wrote my first coherent, intelligible piece when I was in the fifth or sixth grade. I do remember very clearly that by the time I was thirteen I'd written a piece for string orchestra, and it was performed by a very unusual orchestra.

It was a concert by the New Hampshire State Mental Hospital, made up of about 60 per cent local adults from the community, businessmen who wanted to keep their fiddle or oboe playing, and the rest were patients at the mental hospital. So the experience of making music was a wonderful and totally unpredictable one, because frequently these mental patients sort of went off the wall in the midst of rehearsal, the music affected them so strongly. There were never any horrific scenes like *One Flew Over The Cuckoo's Nest*. It was usually a completely out-of-control joyful scene.

But I always look back to that as my first exposure to the social aspects of music making, and I think it's a key one that shows up in my music. There's a lot of unpredictability and room for the unexpected and even bizarre. Maybe it goes back to those evenings in New Hampshire at the state mental hospital.

TS: In an *L.A. Times* article you talk about the death of modernism, that art is moving back to a concern with human values. What do you mean?

JA: You're playing with a loaded gun there. Well, it's foolish to say that modernism is not concerned with human values. Any action that a human being takes is reflective of human values. I think what I was trying to say is that modernism has been very much process-oriented. It has been primarily concerned with revealing the *procedure* by which a work of art is made—examining and exposing materials, whether they be sounds, words, colors or shapes.

What I perceive happening in the arts in the last ten or fifteen years is a movement towards a concern with human psychological values, and with the communication of insight and spiritual values, in the same way that the 19th century artists—Tolstoy and Zola and Wagner and Rodin and Balzac and Dickens—were very much concerned with social issues and with what went on between one person and another. The 20th century and modernism has become somewhat distanced from that. Now we seem to be drifting back in that direction. Certainly my life as a composer has reflected that concern immensely.

And now that I've gotten my feet wet in the operatic world, I feel bitten by the bug for sure. It's a wonderful way in which we can examine important issues of our time and their relationship to human values.

TS: Who are your favorite composers, John?

JA: Everyone. I'm very promiscuous. It depends on the mood I'm in.

TS: Who are they and what makes them great?

JA: I just can't answer that because as soon as I mention a name, I immediately think of fifty others, and have to go on with it. I think it's part of the American experience in a way. I think you can tell that in my own music, that I have a kind of loose filter. A lot of the aural experience of being in America, of constantly hearing music, either in the car or on the radio, wherever you are, filters into your subconscious. I don't buy or collect pop music records at all. And yet just being an American, I'm constantly saturated with it, and it plays a very strong role in the psychic superstructure of my music.

I know I'm very much influenced by the pulsation and the harmonic practice of rock and roll. I couldn't even name a popular rock band, though. I've never listened to it on a conscious level.

TS: Do you think great composers are born or made?

JA: Oh both, of course. You have to be born with that sensitivity for music and work your tail off as well.

TS: Do you think there's a spiritual aspect . . .

JA: (interrupting) What, am I being asked a laundry list here? (laughs)

TS: Well, I want to get all my questions in.

JA: All right. But I didn't get that last one.

TS: Do you think there is a spiritual aspect in great music?

JA: Naturally. Of course.

TS: Are you religious?

JA: No.

TS: What about people like Bach?

JA: Bach was very religious. He was part of the German High Protestant tradition and his life was particularly unique because of his work. He was like a cobbler or somebody who went to work every day and did something. For him it just happened to be the glorification of God through the making of music. So it worked out very well for him.

TS: Does composing come easily, or is it difficult? Do you go through writer's block?

JA: It's very much like being an athlete. When I'm in shape I do it every day. I had to force myself to be very disciplined about it. I'm an early riser, a daytime person. I never, ever work at night. I start work at nine every morning just like a craftsman or somebody going to a job. And I work every day. When I'm not doing it, as now, there's a part of me that's very troubled and restless.

TS: I'm not going to ask you any other questions, social security number or . . .

JA: Thanks. You're the grand inquisitor.

1988

KING SUNNY ADE

A FEW YEARS AGO A UNIQUE, UNCANNY MUSIC KNOWN AS *JUJU* took Europe and the U.S. by storm. Upbeat and fun, its syncopated rhythms turned cool urban hispters into laughing, ecstatic dancers. Juju *was a blend of traditional Nigerian rhythms, electric guitars, and a pedal steel twang reminiscent of country and western music; its prime purveyor was King Sunny Ade. King Sunny, who flies his own plane and dresses in resplendent robes, is a legend in his own country, with well over fifty albums to his credit.*

TS: You were born into a royal family. Didn't that make it difficult to become a musician?

SA: At first, because people are supposed to play music for the royal family, not the family playing music for people. So after leaving grammar school I ran away to a private place and played with some groups there, moving from one to another. When my family went looking for me they didn't find me, but I tried to send a message back home saying I'm okay, I'm safe, I'm doing some research. Then I formed my group. I chose

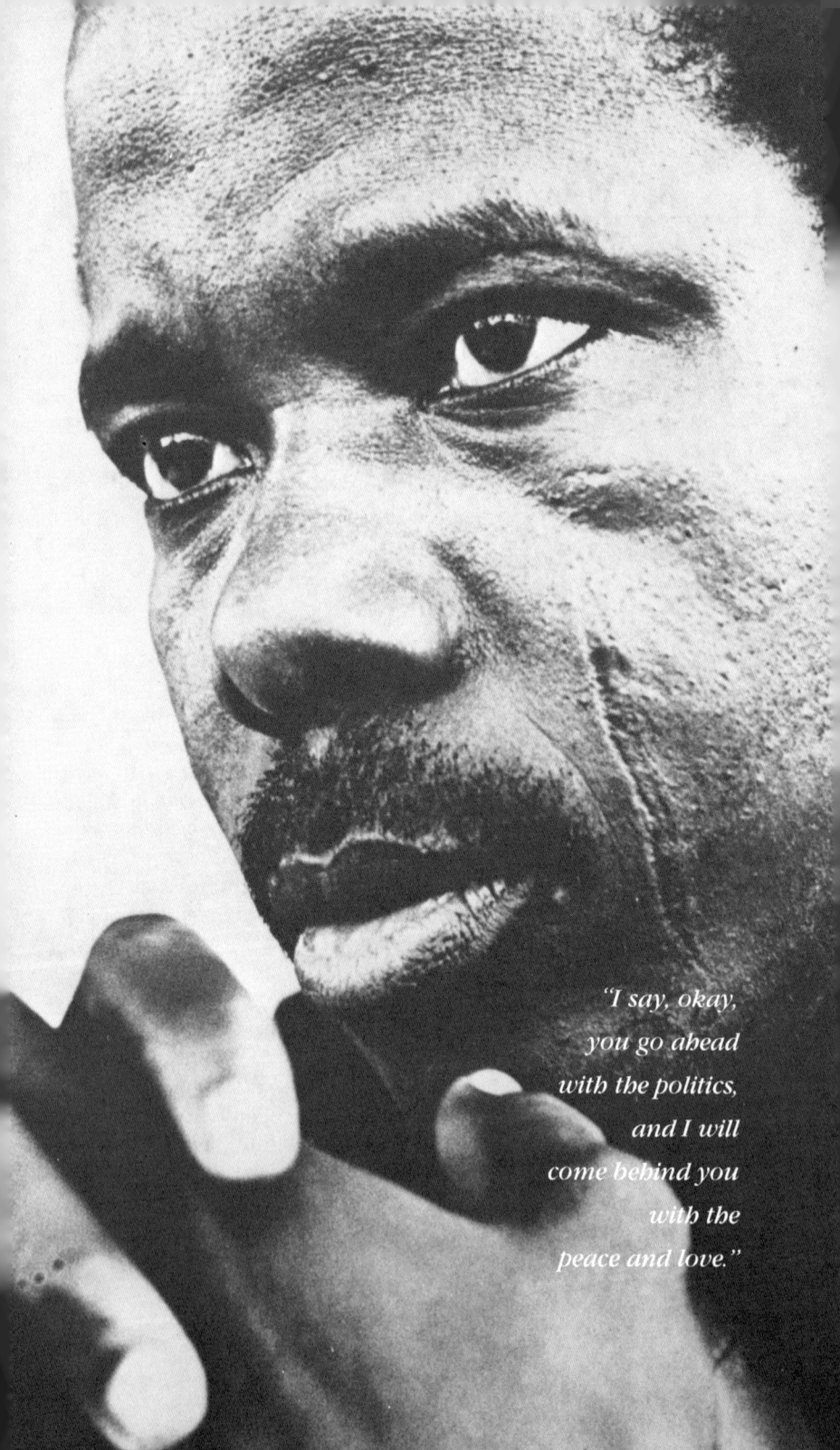

"I say, okay, you go ahead with the politics, and I will come behind you with the peace and love."

my way because I liked music so much.
TS: So you were passionate about music from an early age?
SA: Yes. We had festivals at my grandfather's palace, and a lot of local music surrounding us all the time. I listened to traditional music, and James Brown too when he came in 1963. And I grew up with jazz, because my father loved jazz.
TS: What kind of jazz?
SA: Satchmo. Brubeck. And sometimes my father laid his hands on the keyboards and played some, because he's an organist in the church occasionally.
TS: Did you listen to country and western music too?
SA: Yes, people like Jim Reeves. I so much liked the way he played the pedal steel guitar. I had it in my mind that one day I was going to play sounding like that. So I used my guitar to play his tunes until I saw the actual pedal steel and bought it.
TS: What do you think when you see a record by Paul Simon like *Graceland?* Do you like that record?
SA: Yes, I surely like it because it's paving the way for African music. If we can get more and more people like that involving themselves in African music, eventually it will be one of the biggest musics you can ever find on the planet.
TS: Yet Paul Simon was attacked for making that record, for breaking the cultural boycott.
SA: Well, he actually brought African music and magic together. In fact, I haven't heard him saying on the radio and in the press that he didn't give respect to African music. I cannot attack him personally or on his music. I can only congratulate him for putting African music into his own kind of music and showing it to the whole world. Before you can sell your product to the people who don't know about it you have to demonstrate it. I think this is part of the demonstration, I will call it. And people love it.
TS: You know, Fela Anikulapo Kuti [contemporary Nigerian musician] performed here. You, unlike him, refrain from being openly political in your music. What do you think about Fela? Is it dangerous to be political if you're a Nigerian musician?
SA: No, no. Fela is a good man. He plays good music. He has one

of the greatest bands in Nigeria as well. But everybody has his own line. I don't choose that line. I look at it the way I was born, the way I choose my style, the way I play music. I wasn't supposed to play music, but I personally took it on my own, and it's opposed to my family tradition. I look at the whole world like that. When everybody's taking their line towards the political side of it, I look at it the other way around. I say, okay, you go ahead with the politics, and I will come behind you with peace and love.

TS: Is Prince big in Africa?

SA: Yes.

TS: What do you think of his music?

SA: His music is very good. He has showmanship too, being a young guy, and everybody loves him.

TS: Is Bob Marley venerated just as much as ever?

SA: Yes, because in Africa at the moment they believe he is still alive, though we know he is dead. We believe that his body died but not his name. So he has a lot of fan clubs all over the place.

TS: Are you religious?

SA: Yes, I'm a Christian. I was born into a Christian home. But I don't preach Christianity so far, because I want to play my music around the whole world without having a barrier to any religion. You know, we only have one almighty God, so which way you worship is left to you. It's not necessary that you do certain things, wear a certain dress. I don't believe in that, so I don't carry my religious thing to anybody.

TS: King Sunny Ade, thank you very much.

SA: Thank you for giving me this appointment.
Ashepupo. [Yoruba for "Thank you very much!"]

1987

MOSE ALLISON

MOSE ALLISON HAS BEEN OBSERVING LIFE'S FABLES AND FOIbles *with his funky, offhand wit for over three decades. When I spoke to him he had just come off the road with Van Morrison. Few may know that his wry songs, styled out of the delta blues singers and the great swing bands of the thirties and forties, spring from an informed mind; the composer of "Your Mind is on Vacation and Your Mouth is Working Overtime" is a student of the French skeptics, with a B.A. in literature.*

TS: You are a mythical figure in a way. For every person who's seen you there are probably ten who've heard you, and many who consider you completely unique, as I do, in the world of blues and jazz music. And this all began in Tippo, Mississippi?

MA: Yes. My father was a self-taught stride pianist. He played a little ragtime semi-professionally when he was young—"Sweet Sue," "12th Street Rag," some of those.

TS: He operated the local dry goods store.

MA: Yes, there was a general store with a little bit of everything. Pomade, flour, fatback, work clothes. Mississippi general

STOLEN MOMENTS

*"My philosophy is,
I'm just trying to find the correct blend
of paganism and rationality . . ."*

store, they have a little bit of everything.

TS: What was Tippo like?

MA: It's hard to say. It's sort of like a lot of other colonial outposts around the world.

TS: Was it a heavily segregated town?

MA: Oh sure, definitely. It was ten to one black to white in that area, the Delta. That's where most of the big cotton farms were, so there were a lot of black sharecroppers, some white sharecroppers, a few white landowners. Another world. It wasn't much like what we consider to be urban America.

TS: You didn't start your career as a singer, you started it as a pianist.

MA: That's not completely true, because I sang and played even as a child. My first public performance was at a grade school talent show. I was in the seventh grade and I did Fats Waller's "Hold Tight."

TS: So you were a little advanced.

MA: Yeah. Fats Waller was one of my favorite piano players.

TS: Do you remember any other music that stung you when you were a kid there? Was there live music, or were there "race" stations at the time?

MA: There were radio stations that played primarily blues and stuff, but the main influence on the early years was the jukeboxes. Every store had a jukebox, a Seeburg, and the composition on the Seeburg was about sixty per cent country blues and about ten per cent big band pop music, and the rest was "country," which was referred to as "hillbilly" at that time.

TS: Do you remember some names?

MA: Sure. Memphis Minnie and Tampa Red and Big Bill Broonzy and Roosevelt Sykes. Of course there were always Glenn Miller records here and there, Tommy Dorsey and so forth.

TS: Did you persuade your father to have one of those Seeburgs delivered to the store?

MA: No, we never had one at Allison Brothers Mercantile. But across the street at the Tippo service station they had a hot one, so that's where I used to slip over and play records. But now and then there'd be a guy sitting on the front porch who'd play blues guitar and sing. And people sang when they were in the fields—the whole bit.

TS: You moved to New York in 1956.

MA: But before that I started working in clubs in the South full time, in 1950. The first six-nighter I had was in Lake Charles, Louisiana, and I worked that southeastern Louisiana area for a few months. Mississippi was dry, no whiskey. The clubs had to have illegal whiskey or illegal gambling or whatever, so there weren't too many night clubs in Mississippi. Now on the Gulf Coast, that's a different world altogether. Sort of a spillover from the New Orleans things.

TS: What was it like arriving in New York from Tippo, Mississippi?

MA: Pretty overwhelming. In '51, there was no work, actually. It was one of those periods when there were a lot of jazz musicians and stars walking the streets asking you for five dollars. People you'd been reading about in *Down Beat* for years, you'd see them on the corner looking for a handout. So I went back down South and finished college and worked around for several years, then decided it was time for me to go back.

TS: Mose, your voice gives you away immediately. They say some authors or poets have a certain signature that immediately identifies them. Of course there were a lot of people who said, "I thought he was black."

MA: I heard it so much, I thought I was too. The first time I came to L.A. in 1960, there was a drawn illustrated poster of me as a black person. My hair was a little curlier. (laughs) I remember *Jet Magazine* called me up and wanted to do an article on me one time, and they asked me where I went to college and I told them I graduated from LSU. They said, "Were you the first black man to graduate from LSU?" and I said, "Well, wait just a minute. I think there's something you should know."

TS: Did you develop your voice into a certain sound, or is it what God gave you?

MA: I get just as natural a sound as I can get, as unforced as I can make it. Of course my early influences were the black artists, you know. I remember the first time I heard my voice on tape I was really surprised that I didn't sound like Nat Cole. (laughs) Percy Mayfield was a big influence. I liked him a lot. He had a real loose, unforced style.

TS: One of the things that people perhaps don't realize is that there's a literary aspect to your work. I don't say that in any sort of snobbish way, but some of your lyrics remind me of the French cynics. I guess part of this is a result of the fact that you went to LSU and studied English literature.

MA: Got a B.A. but I missed graduation exercises. I had a job in a honkytonk.

TS: You read a lot and still do, don't you?

MA: Yeah, I'm always reading. In fact, a French cynic is one of my favorite writers. Two of them, as a matter of fact. The early one is La Rochefoucauld, who wrote maxims about self love. If you read La Rochefoucauld you don't need Freud.

TS: And people have also compared you a little bit to Mark Twain.

MA: I get that now and then.

TS: Do you have a philosophy in your songs?

MA: Well, I express it in the songs. One of my favorite words is ambivalence. I think we're drawn to things and repelled by them at the same time. My philosophy is, I'm just trying to find the correct blend of paganism and rationality. I've just about got it figured out that the two things we're capable of are rational acts and paganistic acts. What we have to do is find a balance between those two things. And if we don't start getting more rational pretty soon, the paganistic thing is going to take over.

TS: What about "Middle Class White Boy?" That's the name of one of your records. How did you come up with that idea?

MA: I've gotten a little flak on that. I don't know why. That's a satirical tune. But there have been people who didn't like it, black and white. I don't know why, but I've run across a few people who expressed a little bit of discomfort with the title. I don't think I'm a cynic. I consider what I'm doing as completely positive. Cynics don't have a sense of humor. I consider myself as sort of a deadpan comedian.

TS: You've been very popular in England.

MA: Georgie Fame was my earliest emulator over there. The Yardbirds recorded some of my stuff. Then Brian Auger, and John Mayall, and of course the biggest thing was when The Who did one of my tunes. The most recent is The Clash. They did a tune of mine called "Look Here."

TS: Do you ever go to the South anymore?

MA: Yeah, I still get down now and then. My mother's alive and she still lives in Tippo, and my brother is there, he farms.

TS: Do you ever have a feeling you're going back to your roots?

MA: Well, I like the line Buckminster Fuller came up with. He said, "mammals don't have roots." So I'm not into that roots thing too much. I have strong feelings both ways. I didn't get along that great in Mississippi. I had a lot of opposition and a lot of humiliation. I suppose everybody does. Of course there's a lot I enjoy there, so I'm ambivalent about that whole situation.

TS: Mose, you get on the stand, you're playing a song for the thousandth time, probably. Is there anything you learn playing it again? Do you ever say, "Oh, man, I can't play this tune again but my fans demand it?"

MA: No, I'm glad to get a chance to get to play this tune again. And you know, it's never completely the same twice. There's always that effort, the challenge of putting the music across. That's what it's all about. It's never a given. I don't care if you've been doing it fifty years. You still can't get up there and just sit there and it will happen. You've got to make it happen. People ask me how I want to be introduced. I say introduce me as the man who's in his thirty sixth year of on-the-job training.

1986

LAURIE ANDERSON

Oñe OF THE DECADE'S BIG SURPRISES WAS THE SIGNING OF *experimental performance artist Laurie Anderson to a major recording contract. But well before her "O Superman" became a hit, she was an established art world figure; I remember requesting a bio from Warner Bros. Records and receiving a document an inch thick, detailing her many shows in museums and universities throughout the U.S.*

She has produced large scale media shows and collaborated with a remarkable variety of musicians, among them Peter Gabriel and Phoebe Snow, and writer William S. Burroughs. In person I found her to be friendly and unpretentious, with an impish air of mischief—a sharp, straight talker with nothing of the stuck-up New York artist about her.

TS: "Oh Superman" came from "O Souverain," by Jules Massenet. Where the heck did you get that?

LA: I wrote that song for a friend of mine named Charles Holland, a guy who's probably seventy-one years old, a really great tenor. He used to live in the United States but he's a

"The label 'performance art' is one of those very hazy terms. Nobody really knows what it means, which I like."

black man and couldn't get work here. He used to sing with Fletcher Henderson. So he moved to Amsterdam. Then a guy named Dennis Russell Davies, who's the conductor of the Stuttgart Opera, said, "Charles, we're going to go on tour, back to the United States." I heard this concert in Berkeley that Charles Holland gave. He was so nervous. I mean this guy hadn't been home in forty years. He was dropping his glasses and dropping the music paper, and he couldn't sing.

Finally about midway in the concert he began to sing this song, "O Souverain," which is a kind of prayer, really. It's a real "Lord, help me now" kind of song, a quite beautiful thing by Massenet. And at that point he really began to sing. He did one of the hottest concerts I've ever heard, and then recorded some of that. So I wrote this thing for Charles. [Charles Holland died in 1988]

TS: It reminds me a little bit of a Hungarian pianist named Ervin Nyiregyhazi, a guy who by the time he was around nineteen had conquered every major European city. Then he completely gave it up. He didn't practice. He didn't touch the piano. People wondered what happened to him. Then one day in San Francisco a record producer at some small label was walking by a church and heard this unbelievable piano music coming out. He went in and found this man so many people had been looking for. Nyiregyhazi had been living as a tramp in San Francisco, hitting the bottle heavily and living in one star hotels. Apparently he was married eight or nine times.

To make a long story short, he finally recorded something. He's one of these guys who had a photographic memory, perfect pitch, and also total tactile recall. Once he played something, Lizst or whatever, it would be there forever. Thirty, forty years and he wouldn't need a score or anything—he would go right through it. He did an album for Columbia, I believe.

LA: Quite a story.

TS: Laurie, you were musically trained, but you studied the other fine arts as well. In fact, music is just a part of your performance.

STOLEN MOMENTS

LA: It's a combination of stories, songs, electronics, music, and film. So it's under the label "performance art," which is one of those very hazy terms. Nobody really knows what it means, which I like.

TS: It must be a challenge to get the performance on record. But is there a dimension that's missing?

LA: Well, the records are different kinds of projects than the performances that I do. In the live performances the pictures really comment on the sound. I've tried a few different ways of making that translation, and I'm gradually learning some things about how to do it, I think.

TS: Did it surprise you when "O Superman" took off on the British charts, or did you have a sense that it might hit?

LA: Oh no, it was all planned. Down to the last detail. Uh-huh. (laughs) I think it made it up to the second chair on the charts, and had a brief moment there. It's pretty exciting. I like the fact that younger people seem to like it. That was interesting to me. Also my friends told me that their little kids like it, two-year-olds. I'm interested in those people.

TS: Are you happy to be living now? I've thought that it's a pretty incredible time to be alive in terms of access to history, new electronic instruments, and the media.

LA: Somebody in San Francisco read my palms. I don't know if I tend to romanticize the past, but apparently in my past lives I've been a string of hundreds and hundreds of rabbis. (laughs) I'm a little suspicious, because they go farther back than that. My first life, apparently, was as a cow. Then I was a bird and then I was a hat. Well, the feathers of the bird were made into a hat. And a hat kind of counts as a half-life. (laughs) I don't believe any of this, as a matter of fact. But I don't tend to romanticize the past. I like technology very much. I think that as long as you learn how to use it, it's okay.

TS: Laurie, has literature influenced you?

LA: Sure. But I think now I get more from reading the papers than from books, and from talking to people. The books that I like tend to be pretty current, topical things. I read a lot of art publications also. Basically my background is the art world, so I'm on all those mailing lists.

TS: Do you read the mass-media stuff like *People* magazine, or just the newspaper?

LA: I like data that's a little more raw than *People* magazine. I mean, I like gossip as much as anybody—I probably like rumor more than fact—but I don't read that particular magazine.

TS: You did an album recently with the writers William S. Burroughs and John Giorno. What was it like working with Burroughs?

LA: I'm a big admirer of him and his work. I consider him a kind of very cranky, slightly degenerate Mark Twain-type of guy. His writing is very funny, and very, very precise. He never compromises in terms of exactitude. He's razor sharp. I also like his way of zeroing in on things. He doesn't get into making a lot of generalizations. He doesn't have any cure-alls for modern society, which I'm very suspicious of. It's hard to make some kind of a society that works well. Examples don't really come to mind. I also think that his suspicion of language is interesting.

I've written some songs for him. One is titled "Language Is A Virus From Outer Space," which is a William Burroughs quote. I always thought that was very interesting for a a guy who's written classics in American literature—*Naked Lunch*, and from there on—to say something like "language is a virus from outer space." Language is a kind of disease communicated by mouth, or something. In fact it is a very Buddhist idea, in the sense that there's a thing and yet then you name the thing. In Buddhist thought, that means that there are already too many things. That's also a kind of trick, because sometimes you think that if you can name that thing that you understand it, or if you know somebody's name, that you somehow know them. Burroughs is very keen on making that separation. No, you don't know them because you know their name, or that thing because you know it's name.

TS: I think that Ludwig Wittgenstein once said something like, "Better to see the picture than hear the name."

LA: It's funny, because that's also a quote that's used in that song: "If you can't talk about it, point to it."

TS: You have a lot of fun with language in your songs, and I imagine in your performed art onstage. You don't try to have an exact meaning for things. You allow people to play with your meanings.

LA: Well, it's a slippery system. I love words. I love stories and I love to hear people tell stories. I love the sound of their voices probably more than things written on a page, because then you get so much more information. You get not only what they're saying but their tone of voice. And you can cue into more of what they might mean by what they say. But it's all elaborate guesswork and so much projection on your part. I try not to be real theoretical or didactic. The meanings are loose. It's very important for me to create a situation that's airy enough that people can come to their own conclusions about what those images might mean. They are serious images, not just thoughts on a grid. I'm an artist first of all. So that means I'm working not with ideas but things that you get through your senses first, your eyes and your ears and everything else.

1982

JOAN BAEZ

J OAN BAEZ WAS TO ME A DISEMBODIED VOICE THAT HAD ONCE *filled my parents' house. My sister loved her early Vanguard records, and I remember the sound of that achingly pure soprano coming from the adjacent bedroom.*

When the real Joan Baez entered the studio, I was first struck by her radiant beauty; I suppose I expected more of an ageing hippie in a frumpy print dress than this poised, chic woman who exuded glowing health and could have stepped out of a fashion magazine. As we spoke, I found her funny and straightforward. She had recently been in South America, and our conversation veered, not surprisingly, from music into politics.

TS: Joan, we see a number of folk artists who seem to be disappearing off the scene and coming out with small records on small labels, whereas in the sixties they had albums on big labels. Has the audience in America changed? Do they not want to hear certain things, and just want more of a hedonistic . . .

JB: Sure. I think that has happened, but I think the atmosphere

in this country is changing. It will probably take a couple of years, but there's a tiny budding group of people who are willing to deal with some hope and reality as opposed to just dumping on everything. I mean it's easy enough to dump on everything. The world situation that's been handed down to the youth in this country and around the world is not anything to brag about. But without that gram of hope and caring and concern and willingness to give something, make some sacrifice, or take some risk, then as a human race we may not cut it.

And yet how do you recruit young people to be interested in their own welfare, in the fact that the future is theirs only if they fight for it? That can only be done if you make that fight interesting enough to them that they want to join it, not by scolding them and saying, "You mustn't take dope and hide from reality." That won't work.

TS: I saw the film " Atomic Cafe." The thing that stunned me the most was the incredible naiveté of the American public in the fifties.

JB: Well, the American public is naive, I think. Witness our slow reaction to to the dangers of nuclear war, for instance. Somebody may sincerely believe that deterrence is what's going to save their life, but to even get them to think about it and discuss it is monumentally difficult. It's getting easier now. In Europe it's often discussed, because their parents at least have lived through the war, and they are right in the midst of it. But that's one of the things that's understandable about young people. Who wants to hear that everything you ever knew, and everything that was real to you and around you and in proximity to you, and your relatives and your pets and everything, are going to be fried?

TS: You arrived in Hanoi in 1972, I believe it was, and two days after that, U.S. planes started bombing.

JB: When the first bombs fell they were completely shocked. There hadn't been bombing there for something like six months, and the Vietnamese kept saying, "Excuse me please, go to the shelter, excuse me." I said, "Excuse who?" You know, they were apologizing for the fact that we were

inconvenienced by their being bombed.
TS: People tried to slap you in one ideological camp. It seems to me that your position has been real clear from the beginning, that you're anti-violence and that's basically it.
JB: Well, I would define myself as a non-violent soldier. I mean that's fair enough, because the word non-violence means so little that if you don't put it in some kind of active context it kind of disintegrates. But I've always put myself in situations of conflict and have been active in them. I understand people thinking I was a leftist, because during most of the sixties my activities were against the war in Vietnam, and the right wing wasn't exactly in there pitching with us, you know? To me it was completely consistent to write the open letter to Hanoi condemning the communist government, which is a rotten government, and a lot of the Left was disillusioned and angry and hurt by what I did. But it was the correct thing to do, as far as I'm concerned, and still is. Things are still a mess in Vietnam. We certainly did our share to help the state of affairs in Vietnam deteriorate, because we devastated the place. But then after five years, instead of using the doctors, the architects, all the resources they had, the Vietnamese locked them all up, *a la* USSR, and that didn't seem very helpful.
TS: Did you find Liberation Theology to be alive and well and having an impact in South America?
JB: I'm not sure. It's different in different countries, what role the Church plays. In Chile, it's a fearful business, but many priests will use their parishes as havens for the repressed. In some places it is more openly associating itself with the struggle than other places. I think the only chance that we have of connecting our strengths on behalf of the people who are suffering in Latin America has been through the Church, even in this country, and giving support to people who are willing to speak out at risk to their lives.
TS: Was there anything that you expected to learn from going to Latin America that you didn't? Were there any surprises?
JB: Yeah, there was surprise every single time I wanted to sing and the police told me I couldn't. I always learn massive

amounts of new things. They're always very human. I know about the political structure and the human rights situation —we've read up on all that—but there was the newness of meeting mothers and singing to mothers whose children have disappeared... I'd never really stopped to think about what it would be like to have my child taken away and then not hear a word, to not know whether the child is alive or dead, was tortured or raped, or anything. Then I talked with these mothers about what a nightmare they live in.

TS: Do you think that the U.S. press is doing a fair job in reporting that?

JB: It depends on which press. I think people plug along, trying to give the accurate story. I think we're fighting uphill with an administration that really does not want to criticize human rights in the countries we support and send arms to, and prop up their military. So it's not an atmosphere that nourishes any kind of real understanding of Latin America, the struggle of the people, their sadness and the repression.

1983

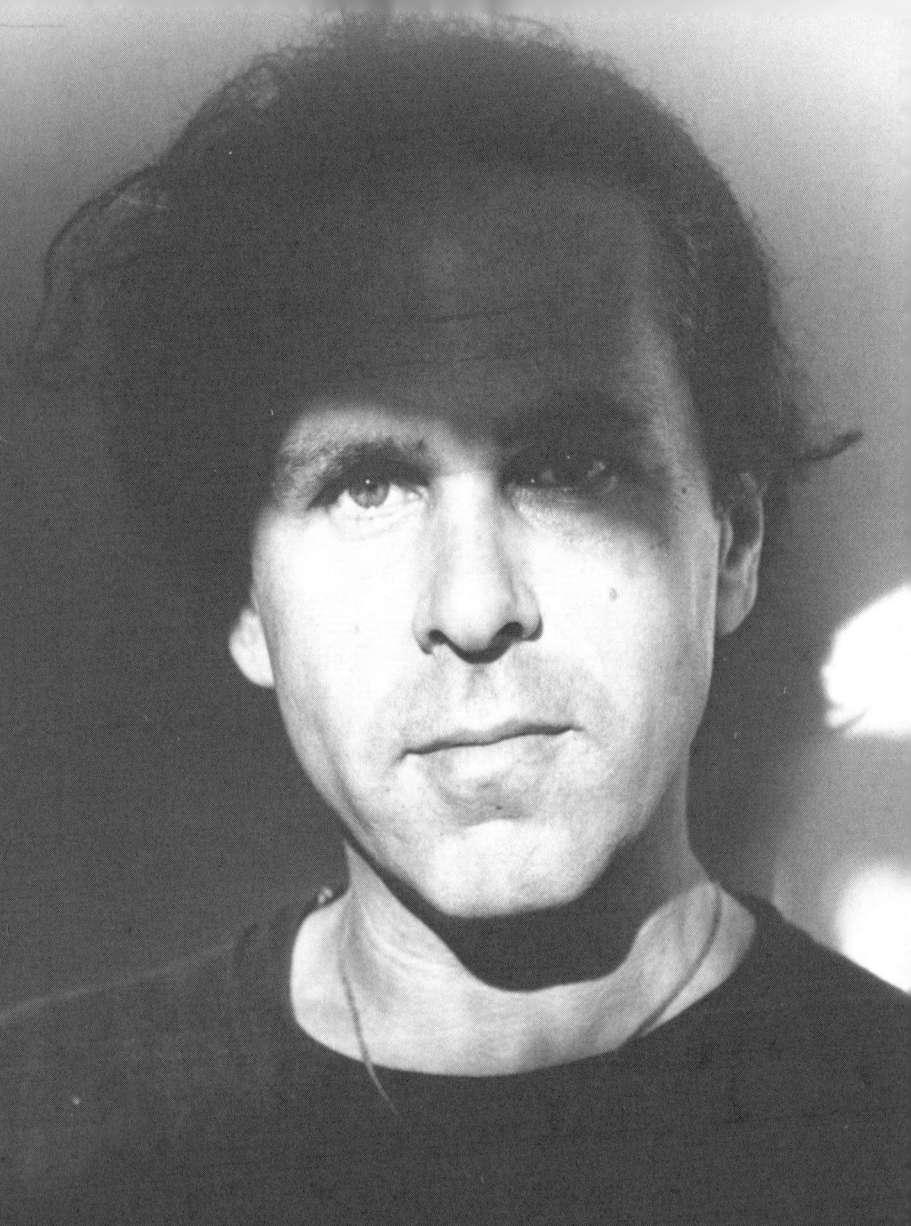

"I dreamed I found a red ruby, a very beautiful stone . . .
That began to represent my heart . . ."

JONATHAN BOROFSKY

IF YOU TOOK ARTIST JONATHAN BOROFSKY'S WORKS AND SEPArated them from each other, you might get individual items that would look like relics for sale from a burned-out sixties hippie on the boardwalk along Venice Beach, or Telegraph Avenue in Berkeley. Taken together in a single installation such as the retrospective at Los Angeles's Museum of Contemporary Art, however, Borofsky emerges with a daring and idiosyncratic brilliance. He shows a profound concern for political and social issues, and as you walk through the exhibition, you can sense the rhythm, cadence, and sheer power of his works. But there's also a sense of play: I never saw children enjoying themselves so much in a museum.

Borofsky has been a musical experimenter as well. Working with composer and synthesist Ed Tomney, the two have composed numerous works in which Borofsky is often found singing or chanting. His "Chattering Man" sculpture and other works also show his interest in the human voice and vocal patterns.

After our hour together, we went out for lunch. During our drive I noticed what a keen observer Borofsky was. He spotted strange writings tacked to telephone poles and construction sites, a pair of *red socks, an odd gait; it seemed that nothing unusual eluded his gaze.*

TS: Music has always been a component of your installations, and that's what we're going to be focusing on. How do the two connect, music and your other work, your drawing and your painting? Does one give you something the other one doesn't?

JB: Oh, definitely. First of all, my work has always been a self-portrait—everything I can pull out of myself expressively. And there is a musical side that has been wanting to come out for some time. I listened to my father play—he's a musician—as I grew up, so I've had that background. I sang in a group too as a teenager. But it was only in the last five or six years that I wanted to incorporate sound into these installations so that people would feel more inside the pieces. It allows me to add another dimension to the exhibition.

TS: When you're struck or moved by something, do you first go to your keyboard, or do you take your pencil out?

JB: Oh, that's difficult to say, really. Different times, different situations. At the moment when I want to relax I seem to go to my four-track rather than to a drawing pad. I enjoy just mixing anything that comes up, starting to play something and putting something against it.

TS: Was there a decision that you made at a certain point that you wanted to become an artist?

JB: No, it started early for me, around ten years old. I started going to the same teacher that my mother took lessons from. Later, painting seemed to be the only thing that was going to get me into a major college. So one thing led to another. From college on, I started to focus on it pretty seriously.

TS: Part of your recent retrospective covers different stages of your career.

JB: It starts with age eight. The first oil painting I did was a little still life with my first teacher. And then age fourteen was where I would take lessons once a week. The idea of the piece is to show the many changes we go through in our lives. As an artist, my work illustrates those changes.

TS: Years ago a bunch of art historians went into... I think it was Borneo, and saw these masks, and told the natives, "Gee, this is great art." And the natives said, "Art? What's that?" What is your idea of art? Is it with a small A? Is it with a big A? That's a big question, I know.

JB: Well, it's a struggle to keep it a small A, because everything around you is shouting big A. "How much money are you making from your art?" "How many shows are you having and who's seen it?" And all that gets to be a little much, when in fact you just want to cultivate the origins of art-making or creativity, which is a private search, a private learning experience. So there's that dualism. It's continuously fought. You're pulling something private out of yourself. At the same time you end up making it very public at the other end of the spectrum. I think the trick is to be able to handle both and make sure you keep that private side available.

TS: Have you always written down your dreams? Did you study Sigmund Freud? How are dreams important for you?

JB: I tell people that I'm a student of the mind. And I'm studying everything that goes on in my mind. That includes when I'm awake and when I'm sleeping. I'm interested in how to improve my mind, all of our minds. Dreams become one component of that study. So I naturally write down everything I can remember in the morning. Later, if it seems like an important dream that might help not only myself but others to see in a larger way, I'll choose to paint it, not in any symbolic way but as directly as I remember it. If I'm riding down the street with my mother, then I'll write that down on the canvas rather than symbolize it.

But again, it's one area that I focus on, just like the politics of the outside world. I try to link up those two, looking for connections between whatever my anxieties and hopes might be, and those of people all around me.

TS: It's been said that your dreams show ambivalence and conflict. How do you respond to that?

JB: Well, some of them do. Some of them are more beautiful. When I have a flying dream, it's a happier moment for me when I wake up because I feel enlightened, like I've been able to rise above the planet. I dreamed I found a red ruby at one point, a very beautiful stone, very shiny and polished. That began to represent my heart for me. So those are positive dreams I hope people are picking up in the show, as well as the ones that are full of anxiety—being chased or struggling with a Hitler-type character, or whatever the repressive force is within me or outside.

TS: I wanted to ask you about your fascination with numbers as well. Music is certainly concerned with numbers. What is that all about anyway?

JB: The numbers began in 1969. I began counting with the number one and writing it on paper—two, three, four, five, six, seven, eight, nine, ten. And then onwards and upwards, towards infinity, filling sheets of paper with the numbers. At the moment I'm on the number two million nine hundred and eighty-four thousand and something. It's taken that many years to get to that number. I don't just do that alone anymore. But I used to just count for a few years and do nothing else.

It's the part of me that likes order, structure, that's looking for the mind to have something very clear and clean to do. Almost like a repetitive mantra. It helps in my case to balance out the side that wants to fly all over the place, have dreams and magic and anything else intuitively that rolls through my head at a given moment that can't be explained. The numbers are very explainable, they're very rational. Ultimately they help me to pull together the many objects in my show that are different.

Each work gets a number written on the corner, and that helps make clear to me the idea that all is one, no matter how disparate the elements are. That can be a metaphor for the planet itself. No matter what our differences, we're still all on one big ball of earth here, floating in space.

TS: What about the man with the briefcase? What about the runner, the chatterer, the hammering man? Who are these characters that figure so prominently in your work?

JB: First of all, they're all portraits of myself in different aspects.

Let's say the hammering man is a worker, the worker in me. The briefcase man is the man in me who carries the briefcase around with my thoughts, my numbers in it. The chattering man is the mind in me that's continuously chattering. However, each one of these is a portrait of everyone else as well. The worker out there on the planet, the chattering mind in you, Tom, or in everyone else, that goes on all day.

TS: What about your show in Berlin? You have different responses in different areas, don't you?

JB: Definitely. It's naturally easier in a country where you speak the same language, because you can speak more about your work to the people and get the feedback. In Berlin it was harder to know what people were thinking. I was only there a few days after I did my shows. I get a good number of people coming up and saying, "This is helpful to me. It's good to see your search," or "I see you're learning to be free. So am I." And that's what it's all about.

TS: Your installations are meant to have a lot of play and a lot of activity and movement. Have you always had them set up that way?

JB: Not quite. It's slowly evolved that way in the last ten years, where I try to bring people more and more in touch with the work, not separate from the painting on the wall. So the installation becomes a total work in itself, and you are inside it. Even inside the work you have the option to pick up a basketball, a ping pong paddle, a speaker and listen to some sounds, become involved. So at one point you are the work instead of separate from the work. You are art.

TS: Do you have any project that you've always wanted to do and haven't had a chance?

JB: I'd like to reach as many people as I can with helpful information. It'll make life happier for all of us. "The Prisoner Tape" was a recent search that I did with Gary Glassman. That's an important step for me. Probably I would evolve it towards something that would reach people on a grander, more mass-media scale. The tape that's playing down at the Museum of Contemporary Art is a fifty-eight minute documentary of interviews with prisoners both in San Quentin prison and women prisoners down here in Chino, talking to them about their lives, asking how they grew up, how they ended up in prison where they're going to spend the rest of their life. I'm trying to find out why people end up like this, with the hope that this will lead to a greater understanding of all of us, how we can become freer human beings.

1986

DAVID BYRNE

I WAS NERVOUS ABOUT INTERVIEWING DAVID BYRNE; I USUALLY AM *when I'm about to talk with a pop icon. The occasion was the release of a curious album,* Music for The Knee Plays, *inspired by theatrical visionary Robert Wilson and New Orleans marching band music. I found the man before me quite thin, contrary to the "big white suit" image I had carried in my head since seeing the film* Stop Making Sense. *David guest-deejayed my show for two hours, with a funny mix of Okinawan pop, Middle Eastern singers, and off-the-wall cuts. In between we talked; he seemed a bit nervous too, and spoke haltingly but with a sly, off-beat humor.*

Afterwards there were people waiting for him in the hall. Some had albums to sign, one had a painting. Then there was the guy who pulled his shirt off, held out a Marks-A-Lot, and asked David to sign his body. I don't remember if he actually did.

DB: I have one of the car buttons on the radio set to this station, those things you pull out and push in.

TS: It's good to have you out there. David, if someone three minutes ago was flipping around the dial and happened to

STOLEN MOMENTS

"There's a record of Eskimo throat singing, where [women] imitate the sounds of blubber frying..."

land on us, and they heard the words of your song "In the Future," from the *Knee Plays* album, they might wonder what the author meant by those phrases.

DB: That's a good question. They all—a lot of them anyway—contradict one another.

TS: "The helpless will be killed." "There'll be no religion." "There'll be no fighting." "There will be a nuclear war." "There'll be no gender differences." "Men will be very masculine, women will be very feminine."

DB: To me they're all very believable. For some of them you have to stretch your imagination, but most of them seem plausible. And yet a lot of them conflict with one another. They couldn't coexist. Or they're opposites. I thought there's some kind of resonance. We can believe in all these visions of the future simultaneously.

TS: You like clipping things out and putting them together.

DB: Uh-huh.

TS: I suppose over a month's time you could clip things from the same newspaper on the same subject, and get a complete list of contradictory statements.

DB: Yeah. (laughs) Although I haven't done that.

TS: Do you read the newspaper?

DB: You know, I don't read the news as much as I used to. I tend to read about the arts and entertainment. I find that the news just gets me upset.

TS: David, you were born in Scotland, weren't you?

DB: Yes, and at the age of two my parents left and they took me with them. They went to Canada where my dad was employed by Westinghouse. Then he moved when I was about seven or eight to Baltimore, where he was also employed by Westinghouse. And that's where I did most of my growing up. It depends on what you think are the formative years. I thought high school and junior high were when I started to form my tastes and make decisions about what I was going to do.

TS: Did you have a band in high school?

DB: Yeah. It was when The Beatles and The Rolling Stones and The Temptations and all that was popular. I was briefly in a band for about a year or so. We played the current songs that everybody would play—"Satisfaction" and "You Really Got Me" and stuff like that. Then we disbanded but I continued to play. I checked a lot of records out of the library so my tastes could be more eclectic, and I didn't have to risk my allowance on stuff.

TS: A lot has been made about Talking Heads being an art rock band, following the tradition started by Velvet Underground. Has that become a cliché? Does that mean anything any more to you?

DB: Well, I don't know what it means any more. It can annoy me when it's kind of implying that it's a game for us, or that we don't have sincere feelings about our music. When that's kind of the subtle implication in the term "art rock," then I try to avoid it.

TS: David, can you recall the strangest music you ever heard?

DB: There's a record of Eskimo throat singing. Women making sounds to one another, where they imitate the sounds of their environment, like the sounds of blubber frying. Or the sound of ice breaking up. And they imitate it with their voices. Or not exactly. I mean it's not like "eurw eurw eurw" (makes sound of ice breaking), but it's a very stylized kind of imitation. That's a very strange kind of thing, very different from anything we can think of.

TS: Is there any one item that you hear first when you listen to a piece of music?

DB: I think there's always an attitude, a sensibility that comes across with music. And everybody experiences that. I guess that hits me right away. Then later on it becomes apparent, the various parts, the arrangements or whatever.

TS: Is your life getting more and more hectic?

DB: It does in bursts. There are weeks when it gets really, really hectic. Then I manage to slow things down, take control of things, and it becomes manageable again.

TS: What do you do to make things manageable?

DB: Leave town. (laughs) I just left New York. Things were getting really hectic.

TS: Do you like the pace of New York City life? Are you an urban person?

DB: I think so. I like the countryside but I find there's an energy in urban places that I guess comes from the interaction of people that can be inspiring.

TS: Thanks for coming down and guest deejaying this morning. Sorry there aren't any openings here.

Discography of LP's deejayed by David Byrne:

"Elastic Dance" from *My Life in a Hole in the Ground.* African Head Charge.
Ry Cooder with the Okinawan band Bloodline.
Abafana Baseqhudeni, or The Cockerel Boys. Cuts: "The Bad Neighbor" and "Every Friday."
Music from Fellini's *Casanova.* Nino Rota.
The Tango Project. "La Cumparsita."
The McGarrigle Sisters. "Complainte for Old Saint Catherine."
The Catherine Wheel. David Byrne/Twyla Tharp. Cuts: "Ade" and "Walking."
Ladysmith Black Mambazo from *Induku Zethu.*
The Dirty Dozen, "Caravan," from *My Feet Can't Fail Me Now.*
"Tree," and "I've Tried" from *Music for the Knee Plays.* David Byrne/Robert Wilson.
Penguin Cafe Orchestra. "Music for a Found Harmonium" from *Broadcasting From Home.*
Robert Wyatt, *Shipbuilding.*
John Cale, *Helen of Troy.* Cut: "I Keep A Close Watch."
Hank Williams, "Howling At The Moon."

1985

"Police came on stage with shotguns and said, 'That's the end of the show, because white members of the band don't have a permit . . .'"

JOHNNY CLEGG

WHILE JOHNNY CLEGG WAS ONE OF THE FIRST MUSICIANS TO bring the infectious rhythms of South African music to America, it was his bi-racial group Johnny and Sipho, and later the larger group Juluka, that brought down the wrath of the authorities in South Africa. His latest group, Savuka, has released two hit albums and is drawing more people to South African music. His riveting description of his odyssey through the battleground of South African musical culture provided a powerful reminder of the political threat posed by the simple act of musicians getting together to make music.

TS: How did you wind up in southern Africa?
JC: I was born in England in 1953. My mother divorced my father when I was six months old and we returned to her place of birth, which was then Rhodesia. I grew up on a farm there. My mother remarried a South African journalist, and we immigrated to Johannesburg when I was seven. We stayed in Johannesburg for two or three years and then we immigrated to Zambia for a little while. Spent two years

there schooling. Then we returned to Johannesburg, after which I stayed there permanently up until now. So I've got quite a checkered background in that regard, having schooled both in Zimbabwe, Zambia and in South Africa.

TS: Did you always want to become a musician?

JC: No, I never wanted to become a musician. My mother was a cabaret singer and was very involved with music. I didn't particularly like the people she hung around with as a youngster. I found I had nothing in common with the night club scene. I was really turned on to acoustic folk music, Celtic folk music, traditional stuff. Then when I was twelve, thirteen, I met Zulu street musicians in Johannesburg who were playing and tuning the guitar in a really crazy way, playing rhythms and melodies which in a certain sense are quite reminiscent of the Celtic music that I'd been listening to up until then. I started playing with them, bought myself a guitar, and after one and a half years became completely involved with the Zulu migrant labor street music community.

I developed a very strong friendship with a particular migrant, Sipho Mchunu, who I played with for about six years, from 1970 to '76, before we recorded our first singles as Johnny and Sipho. Three years later we formed the band Juluka. In the early years, obviously, we played strictly traditional Zulu music.

TS: The album *Rhythm of Resistance* [taken from the BBC documentary of the same name] brought you fame and notoriety in South Africa, because with Sipho you were the first mixed group, correct?

JC: Well, I don't think we were the first mixed group. I think if we look back to the fifties, there was quite a strong multi-racial tradition, especially in the African jazz music scene. It was the sixties when the cultural segregation really became serious. I think we were the first multi-racial grouping, if you want to call it that, experimenting with culture in the sense of looking at the roots of Zulu culture and, say, Celtic folk music and trying to find threads of similarity, trying to weave them somehow into a meld or a mix. The band Juluka was the first band in South Africa to effect a full mix of tribal music and Celtic folk music. Later we mixed in general Western pop, from jazz to blues and reggae.

So we came out of a pretty stifling period, the Vorster period of the sixties where the radio stations were segregated first on a racial basis—that is, black, white, Indian—and then those were further segregated on an ethnic basis. So if you were a white person you had to tune into an English radio station or an Afrikaans radio station. If you were a black person you had ten different tribal stations to tune into. We started to mix the languages on record. We broke ground on that level as well. Language is a very, very politically charged issue in South Africa. We mixed Zulu and English, which of course really upset the programming on radio because people would say, "Is this a Zulu record or an English record?" And we suffered for that on the SABC [South African Broadcasting Corporation].

The period coming out of 1969-70-71 was a period where cultural apartheid was very strictly enforced. Sipho and myself could not play in public anywhere. We played alternative venues in Johannesburg, migrant labor hostels. There was a very strong street music tradition which you found on the rooftops of apartment blocks. Many flat cleaners were street musicians. So on the weekends we would go onto the rooftops of these buildings and congregate and mix and play there.

We also played in gambling dens, speakeasies. And there were certain street corners in the industrial side of Johannesburg where the migrant labor hostels were situated, where out in the street on a weekend you could actually meet other musicians and play. But we were never allowed to play anywhere near the city hall or any kind of public area. And that started us playing together in 1970. After the June riots in 1976 there was a reaction from the government to give certain concessions on a social and cultural level. They began to open up certain venues for multi-racial performances, although these were very limited in the beginning. There were ridiculous rules, like if there were blacks and whites on stage there could only be one racial group in the audience. Or if there were many racial groups in the audience, there could only be one racial group on stage.

It was crazy. And we went through that for about a year to eighteen months. Then it basically became open to everybody. But these open-to-everybody venues were also few and far between, and strictly controlled. It opened up a lot more for us around 1982, 1983, when more and more concessions were given on a social and cultural level, to the point where now at the end of 1987, there's a belt of venues which runs through South Africa, mainly in the built-up areas, where multi-racial performances are quite common. However, in the more conservative areas, in the Northern part of the Transvaal, in many parts of the free state, you tend to find that you go back twenty years in time. We often find we cannot perform there because they do not allow black people into the city hall or into the normal sort of venues.

TS: You are an honorary Zulu. What does that mean?

JC: Well, I wouldn't quite put it like that, but I have a special relationship with four clans. The Zulu in fact are a language group very much—if you want to conceptualize them—like the Scottish, in a way. They're a group of clans who are fiercely independent of one another, brought together by a common language and culture. But the clans themselves are very powerful bodies. They have their own rituals, their own history, and in a way, their own little subcultures. Over the period of the past twenty-odd years I've been incorporated into four clans, in a ritual relationship. They have certain claims and obligations over me and I have certain claims and obligations towards them. The clans in particular are the clans of Sipho, the Chunu people, the clans of Ndlovu, which is the clan of the dancer-percussionist who works with us in Savuka, and the clan of Qoma, who's a very special friend of mine. He's a man who makes car tire dancing sandals for Zulu war dancing teams in Johannesburg. He makes his living from this. He's known as Bafazane. I wrote a song for him called "Bullets for Bafazane", during the Juluka period. And also with the clan of the Ngele people. These people were very good to me when I was conducting research into the origins of a particular dance style which I was investigating for my M.A. degree.

The claims and obligations are essentially that as a clan member I'm obliged to see that if any young member of a clan who arrives in Johannesburg is in trouble, or in jail, or needs a job or has been arrested, or has a problem, or needs money to get back home, or needs to use the phone or whatever it is—he knows that there's a clan member there. Myself the same way, if I require assistance in any way. Also during certain festivities and ritual celebrations in Zululand, I'm obliged to be present at these festivities, whether it's a Christmas celebration, a New Year's celebration, or a slaughtering for the ancestors.

It all sounds very serious, but it's also a lot of fun. We're all age mates, which means we're peers, and that's a very important principle in Zulu society, the age principle. Because you grow old together in the world and you're part of an age regiment.

TS: Does this ever bring on problems with the police?

JC: In the early days, obviously, I got into a lot of trouble. My first arrest was for trespassing into a black area. In fact it was a municipal compound where the Zulu migrant workers were living. Subsequently I was arrested in all these other alternative venues that I mentioned before—compounds, apartment block rooftops, migrant hostels—even in Zululand itself, when I went to visit Sipho's family to meet them. I knew him for about a year and a half and I really wanted to meet his family. We went down there, and after three days the security police arrived and threatened to deport me back to England. Sipho was charged and brought to trial for bringing a white man illegally into a tribal area, which is considered to be a security zone by the police. Sipho won the case on a technicality, saying that there wasn't a sign. In all these areas there used to be a very big green board with white lettering saying, "You are now entering a black area. Anybody with white skin has to have a government permit." And there was no board, so he got off.

We had a lot of that kind of harassment, at shows as well. We had shows stopped in Nigel, in the townships where we played. Police came on stage with shotguns and said, "That's the end of the show, because white members of the band don't have a permit to be in the township." But all in all, I think you grow up in a situation like that and you don't have anything to compare it with. You deal with it, you know, you go through with it. And of a hundred percent of shows, fifteen to twenty percent you'll have a bit of a hassle. You'll go through some ugly moments but you'll get eighty percent done and that's okay.

TS: Do you think that Nelson Mandela will be released?

JC: I think it's definitely going to happen within the next two or three years. There are a lot of problems surrounding this because certain groupings in the broad democratic movement inside as well as outside South Africa feel that they don't want to get involved in tokenism. There are many political prisoners in South Africa who have been in jail as long as Nelson Mandela but who are not as famous and who don't have the kind of public profile that Nelson had. There's a feeling that there should be some form of total amnesty given to all political prisoners, because if in principle if you release one, then why not release everybody?

So we do know that Nelson has been holding out and saying, "I don't want to leave without the rest of my brothers and sisters leaving." So there is where the issue is going to settle, I think. I think the government would clearly have loved to just release Nelson Mandela and reap the benefits of the international publicity from that. And I think that people in the broad democratic movement are aware of that and would like to communicate what that release is generally worth to the democratic movement. Because we have many organizations banned, many people in jail, many people in detention. I think that's the issue, not just the individual case.

TS: Have you seen *Cry Freedom* yet?

JC: Yes. I had a mixed reaction. I think Attenborough had a very difficult task to accomplish. One was to give a good account and deal properly with the incredible life story of Steven

Biko. At the same time he wanted to put together a political adventure movie. I think there was a bit of a problem in the flow of the movie, from that angle. I felt that one of the most dramatic things for the whole of South Africa in that period was the actual trial, the court scene. I think a lot more could have been done with it, because the incredible brutality and the consciously cold-minded attitude of the police at that time was brought to the fore. That kind of a problem is difficult to overcome.

The movie wasn't essentially about Biko, it was about Donald Woods. And from that point of view, as a kind of South African political adventure movie I think it carries itself quite well. It definitely gives you a feel of what's going on there and what was going on in that period. I recommend that everybody see that movie. It's for people who want to get a general feeling of the quality of the struggle there. But I don't think it's a great movie if you want to understand Biko's life or the issues that his particular story brings out. His story highlights the South African situation. You must remember he's the only person who died in political detention and was legally proven to have died as a result of police actions. That's why he's a very important political rallying point.

TS: Well, Attenborough certainly made a statement at the end of *Cry Freedom* with the list of names—"Fell on a bar of soap," "Died while climbing," "Fell on stairs,' again and again.

JC: Yes, well the sixties especially were a terrible period. The tenth floor of the police building became notorious. People were constantly jumping out of the window, falling from the stairs and things like that. It was a dark period of South African history. But even at this moment, with the state of emergency, there have been some equally brutal and brutalizing situations on both sides. Whether it's necklacing . . .

TS: Necklacing?

JC: Well, the angry young kids in the township, if they suspect anybody of being an informer or collaborator—and of course, the definition of a collaborator is so broad and so undefined—that innocent people have been killed. A necklace is basically a tire which is put around somebody and petrol thrown over the person and burnt. There was a chaotic period where the incredible anger of the young people and the feeling of desperation and frustration at the situation boiled over. The anger of the young people is a direct result of the government's repression and its failure to dismantle apartheid. Whether it's in the form of mass detentions, interrogations, or the harsh measures imposed by the state-of-emergency regulations, young black people have had to endure one of the darkest periods of struggle.

TS: What do you think is going to happen in South Africa? Do you think it's a time bomb that's going to go off? Is there a solution?

JC: No, I don't think there's a time bomb that's going to go off. I think we're in the middle of a revolution. We aren't going to see—well, in the foreseeable future anyway—the kind of guerrilla warfare that went on in the other front line states in their liberation. I think South Africa is a specific case of a highly industrialized country where the white settler community has sufficient numbers to actually control. They also have a highly sophisticated military and intelligence set-up. There's also a sufficient amount of competition and confusion between different liberation groups within South Africa for the military option to not be that successful, I believe.

I think the road to emancipation there is going to be through the trade union struggle. It's the trade unions who are in fact organizing communities, pushing for rights, raising many issues and taking them on. It's going to be that kind of a struggle, a legal struggle, a civil rights struggle, accompanied, obviously, by bursts and flares of violence and urban guerrilla warfare.

1987

LEONARD COHEN

I STAYED UP LATE THE NIGHT BEFORE PREPARING FOR MY CON-
*versation with the gravelly-voiced poet who always seemed to
keep his knife sharpened in his lyrics. I hoped he wouldn't turn
that knife on me.*

*When he walked in I was struck by how good-looking he was. My
anxiety was disarmed somewhat by his gentle handshake and the
kindness in his eyes. I had no doubt, after repeated listenings, that his
new LP,* I'm Your Man, *was a masterpiece: dramatic, caustic, comic.
Thirty minutes was little time to explore twenty years of work, but I
jumped at the chance to talk with this gracious and fascinating man.*

TS: Did it surprise you that this new album has been so successful?

LC: Well, you hope but you never expect.

TS: Do you take it as a compliment that you're more popular in Europe than in America?

LC: I'm grateful to have an audience anywhere. The audience in Europe is wide. I seem to have struck deep into some of the countries. I have small pockets of listeners in America. I like

STOLEN MOMENTS

*"The kind of surrender that is
involved with love means that
you have to take a wound also..."*

singing in the United States because my language comes out of this language and people can follow the real meaning of the songs. I use the cadences and rhythms of the American language. I know that in Norway, for instance, or in Scandanavia where English is a second language, there still is some kind of translation process going on.

TS: Do you identify more with a European cultural tradition of songwriters—Jacques Brel, Mikos Theodorakis, Georges Moustaki, Brassens?

LC: Of course those singers and songwriters have meant a good deal to me. But so does Chuck Berry.

TS: Did growing up as a Jew in Montreal during World War II affect your songwriting?

LC: I suppose everything is part of the composite. It was a very privileged position that I grew up in, so it was only toward the end of the war that I really understood what was going on during it. The only deprivations we suffered was that we couldn't get American bubble gum, and the comics weren't in color. We were very protected from the reality.

TS: Were you brought up in a traditional Jewish home?

LC: Yes, and a family very involved in the community, in establishing hospitals and synagogues, a free loan association. My grandfather founded the first Anglo-Jewish newspaper in North America.

TS: I was wondering how your songs reflect your own view of yourself, as a songwriter and a musician.

LC: It's very hard for me to locate a view of myself. It's one of the things I'm least interested in. I'm reminded of that story I read in *Dalva,* a novel by Jim Harrison, who is speaking of certain tribes where the white man tried to introduce the mirror, and certain native American tribes refused to accept the mirror. The reason was, they said, that your face is for others to look at.

TS: Is songwriting for you a lonely craft?

LC: That hardly begins to describe it. It's a desperate kind of activity. I don't know why it should be that way, but it is. It seems to take an enormous effort to bring work to completion.

TS: Do the words come first, or do you hear the music?
LC: It's generally some uneasy marriage of those two elements. A phrase will come, or a chord change. Then you'll get maybe the first verse with music and words, but then as the words change the musical form has to change. It usually takes a couple of years to bring a song to completion.
TS: Do you get tired of hearing "Suzanne?" Would you listen to it if it came on the radio when you were driving your car?
LC: I think that would be the only occasion that I'd listen to it. Well, I don't listen to any of my work. I don't even have a player. I have a little Walkman. I usually have to buy them every couple of months. I leave them in hotel rooms.
TS: Is it more important for you to be recognized as a poet or as a musician?
LC: Well, depending on how isolated you feel, any kind of recognition is welcome.
TS: In reading your bio, I was wondering what motivated you to leave your Greek island of Hydra and head for Nashville, Tennessee. Was it to gain wider exposure of your poetry, or just to make money?
LC: There was certainly an economic aspect. I'd been living on an island on the Mediterranean for some time—never completely, I'd always have to come back to Canada to put some money together—but I was living for a thousand dollars a year there. I'd come back to make a thousand dollars and my boat or plane fare then go back for as long as that would last. I wrote a lot of books there and a lot of songs. At a certain point I just felt like changing. When I moved back to Canada I published a novel, *Beautiful Losers,* which got a lot of stunning reviews, but I couldn't even pay the rent. In hindsight it seems like the height of folly—you know, I'll take care of my financial problem by becoming a singer. But I got ambushed in New York by the so-called folk song renaissance that was going on there. It did take care of the financial problem, actually.
TS: How did John Hammond [renowned record producer] hear about you?
LC: John Hammond was an extremely gracious man. Someone

arranged an introduction. I was living at the Chelsea [Hotel] and he said, "Would you like to play me some songs?" We went back to my room and I played him seven or eight songs and he said, "You got it."

TS: People have been talking about your voice ever since your early songs. Is it the voice that God gave you or did you work in a certain way to develop your . . . golden voice?

LC: I think in my first record I had a voice that was appropriate to the songs. Then I think I got lost for a long time. I think that now in the last two records I've begun to find the voice that represents me. But it's not a strategy. I think it's cigarettes and whiskey.

TS: I remember reading in an interview that you said that rather than having a dark cast of mind you were merely realistic. Do you think reality is dark?

LC: I think it participates in all the shades. But I think that people have an appetite for seriousness. And seriousness is neither light nor dark. It's just the way it is, and there's a great nourishment when you just name the thing as it is. I think there are certain occasions where cynicism is appropriate. One should be cautious.

TS: Has your view of romance changed over the past twenty years, since you embarked on your songwriting career?

LC: Well, I think that it changes naturally, but I think that the position I took in some of those early songs is not so far from the position I take now.

TS: Which is?

LC: That the kind of surrender that is involved with love means that you have to take a wound also.

TS: Do you think that it's a typical growth process, or that it's more your own?

LC: I can't believe that my predicament is unique.

1988

"People my age come in to see me, people who listen to the punk and the contemporary... but also have found another musical choice."

MICHAEL FEINSTEIN

NEW YORK THEATER CRITIC CLIVE BARNES HAS CALLED MI-
*chael Feinstein "the most distinctive classic pop singer of his
generation." Behind the boyish looks and onstage exuber-
ance of this young singing and piano whiz lies a mastery of the great
American standards written long before he was born. He's an
anachronism. While others in his generation were listening to the
Beatles and Stones, Michael Feinstein was delving into the wit and
nuance of Porter, Berlin, and Rogers and Hart.*

TS: Well, you must be about thirty now.

MF: Recently turned thirty, yes.

TS: You look like you're about twenty one, the sort of guy who must get carded going into clubs. Have you always had this attraction for songs that were written so long before you were born?

MF: I always had an attraction to this particular kind of music. I didn't know when the music was written. My parents played these songs when I was growing up, but I didn't know they were old songs. I just knew they appealed to me more than the contemporary music on the radio. So it was an involvement that began when I was very young.

TS: So you're running around in junior high school and saying, "Wow, I've just discovered this new song by Cole Porter!"

MF: Yes, and my friends were saying, "Yeah, but what about the Beatles?" (laughs) It was very strange. I had to hide my Bing Crosby records when friends would come over to my house. They couldn't believe it.

TS: When you were twenty years old you met with Ira Gershwin. What happened? You've been called his protegé.

MF: I met Ira Gershwin through Mrs. Oscar Levant, June Levant. Less than a year after I moved to Los Angeles, I met June through a series of coincidences. She was very impressed with my knowledge of the Gershwin era, and eventually effected an introduction to Ira Gershwin. When I met Mr. Gershwin he was eighty and I was twenty. I think he was impressed with the fact that I knew so much about his work. I was part of a generation that he thought had passed him by. He asked me to start working for him, taking care of his archive of Gershwin memorabilia. I started cataloguing his voluminous collection of phonograph records, and then moved on to other types of memorabilia and archival material in his home. I eventually spent six years taking care of that material, and along the way I became very close with Ira.

TS: You sing songs by quite a few great composers. If you had to give a brief verbal description characterizing some of them, could you come up with a word or two?

MF: I'll try.

TS: George and Ira Gershwin.

MF: Well, I think that the Gershwins are probably my favorite show composers. George Gershwin certainly created a bonding between the jazz world and the show music world, and he created a new sound in show music that changed the face of music for the entire world. Of course when George Gershwin wrote *Rhapsody in Blue* in 1924 it was the most amazing thing. He was only twenty five, going on twenty six, when he wrote the piece. And people considered him just a tunesmith. He was, in my opinion, the greatest American composer we've had. And Ira certainly was a genius with his lyrics but very rarely acknowledged as such.

TS: What about Irving Berlin?

MF: I think Irving Berlin is the grandfather of show music. Irving Berlin and Jerome Kern were the ones who most influenced Gershwin, Burton Lane, Harold Arlen and even Vernon Duke, who came to the United States from Russia in 1924. They really set the ground rules for a lot of show music, for the form of a lot of theatrical songs. Berlin was one of the charter members of ASCAP, the songwriters' society that was formed in 1914. He's underestimated as a lyric writer. People consider him a great composer, but people tend to discount his ability as lyricist.

TS: Cole Porter.

MF: It's said all the time, but he certainly was the most sophisticated and witty lyricist. He was very risqué, and a lot of his lyrics were banned from the airways at the time they were created. They were too honest in the emotions they expressed at a time when people didn't want to know about some of those things. He was certainly the most brilliant.

TS: Steven Sondheim.

MF: I suppose Steven Sondheim is our most important theatrical composer today. I love to sing Sondheim's music. I'm a little irritated when people are always saying that his melodies are not up to snuff or that they're too difficult for the mass audiences. I think that in the next several years people are going to become more and more aware of Sondheim as a man with great ability for writing wonderful melodies.

TS: And finally, Rogers and Hart.

MF: Well, I suppose I prefer the work of Rogers and Hart to Rogers and Hammerstein. Larry Hart—it's amazing that he was able to turn out brilliant rhymes very quickly. Larry Hart would write a dummy lyric before he wrote his finished lyric to get an idea of what sort of form the lyric would have to take for a song. I love his dummy lyric for "There's A Small Hotel," where his original lines were, "There's a girl next door/Who's an awful bore/Really makes you sore/To see her . . . Bye and bye perhaps she'll die/Perhaps she'll croak this summer/Her old man's a plumber/She's much dumber ..." He wrote those nonsense lyrics so he would know where the rhymes would fall. He learned that he had to write the song with triple line rhyme—summer, plumber, dumber, that sort of thing. He was wonderful.

TS: Are great songwriters becoming an endangered species, Michael?

MF: No. I think venues, outlets for the great songwriters are in some ways endangered. But I think there's an awful lot of material. They just don't have too many opportunities to be heard. Yet I also feel that there is a strong renaissance of the material of the great composers—the Gershwins, Kern—not because it's old or nostalgic, but because it has important values for today's world. It's wonderful to have people my age coming in to see me, people who listen to the punk and the contemporary, the rock stuff, but also have found another musical choice. It's very gratifying to know that people are turning back to this music.

1987

PHILIP GLASS

A S I SIT IN RAPT ATTENTION LISTENING TO PHILIP GLASS TALK *about music, I can't fail to notice how much he enjoys it. He has been the subject of scathing reviews and innumerable jokes: "Knock knock." "Who's there?" "Knock knock." "Who's there?" "Knock knock." "Who's there?" "Philip Glass." But along with earlier pioneers like Terry Riley and La Monte Young, Glass has helped forge a new type of experimental music far removed from the academic style of other contemporary composers, and his concerts are packed with pop-chic crowds. He seems to be equally at home composing controversial extravaganzas such as* Einstein on the Beach *and* Akhnaten, *scores for films such as* Koyaanisqatsi, *or music to songs by Suzanne Vega and Linda Ronstadt. He is the first CBS Masterworks artist since Igor Stravinsky and Aaron Copland to be offered a lifetime contract.*

TS: Do you think there's a particular flavor or mood to the music of the 1980's?

PG: Well, I do, actually, though it's taken us a while to figure out what that is. For one thing, I see a lot of "theater" kinds of

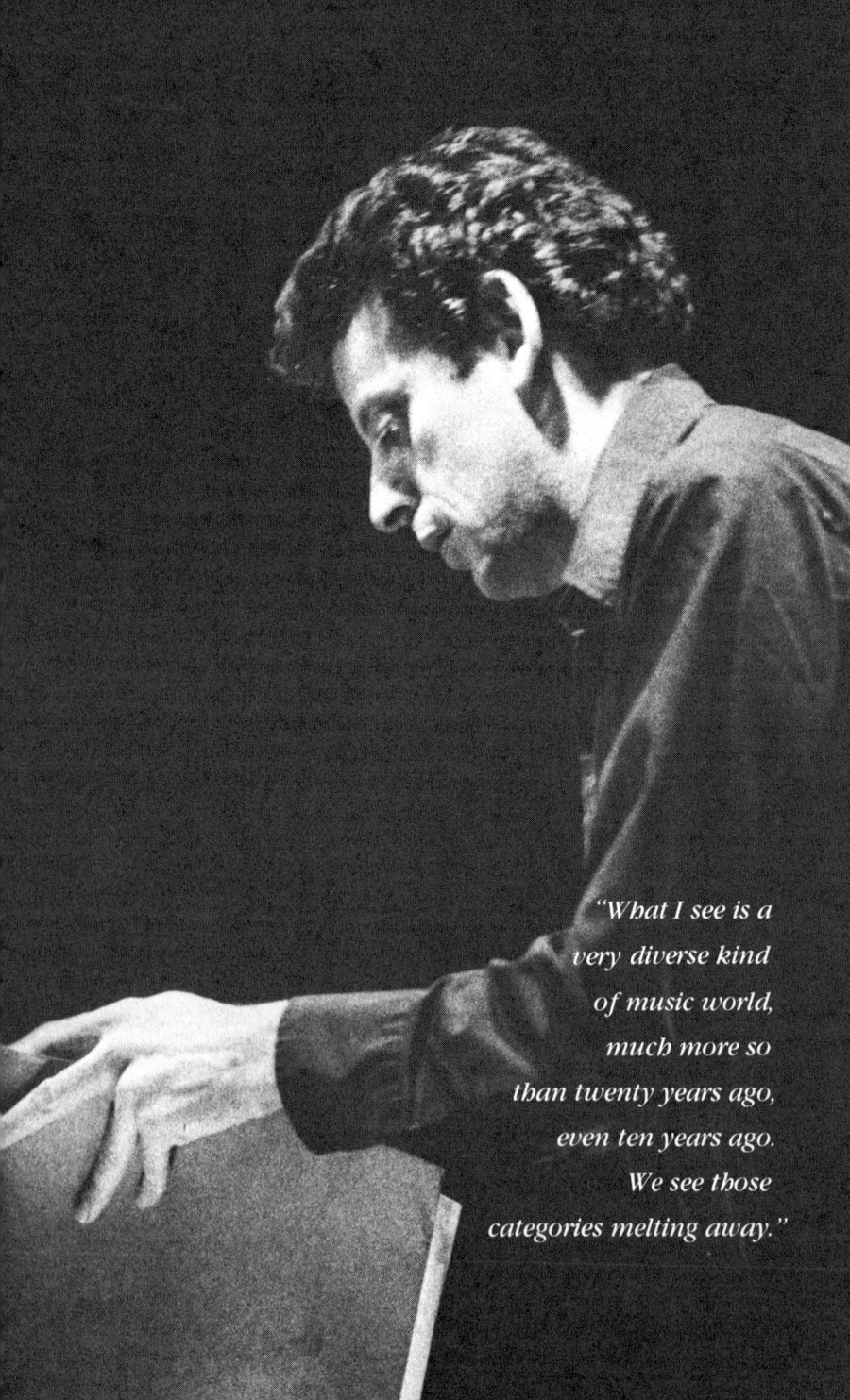
"What I see is a very diverse kind of music world, much more so than twenty years ago, even ten years ago. We see those categories melting away."

pieces being done. I can think of seven or eight people writing theater pieces right now. We see a lot more collaborations between musicians and dancers and designers. People are becoming much more comfortable with technology. We see a lot of things that are synthesizer- or computer-related happenings in music, and it's not such a big deal any more. What I see is a very diverse kind of music world, much more so than twenty years ago, even ten years ago. Once again we see people working in experimental areas, whether it's jazz or rock or new music. Sometimes it's the same people. We see those categories melting away. So you have people like the Kronos Quartet. They'll play Thelonious Monk and a new piece by Jon Hassell and a new piece by myself. That's also something new.

TS: Are you excited by life in the 80's? I imagine you are.

PG: I'm real busy, so I'm excited. It's been real good for me.

TS: Back in the forties, fifties, sixties, people looked ahead to the future. But now people seem a little apprehensive about that.

PG: Do you think that's because they can see the edge? (laughs)

TS: Well, I guess I'm thinking of the nuclear side, the dark side of technology.

PG: I think there's that. If you grow up with children—I've been living with my children for the last seventeen years—you see it from that point of view. There's no doubt that we see the world differently generally, and that affects how we see it culturally. You began this program with music from two different parts of the world, and in many ways it's very clear what the relationship is. It's not hard to figure out why you played those two pieces of music together. We see the world as a much smaller place. Because it's much smaller there's much more diversity, which creates terrific interest and terrific problems. That comes with it. I don't think there's any way to have that kind of plurality without the problems that you get into—ecological or social or whatever. But they're there. It makes a very creative atmosphere for people to work in. I don't know why it should be, but it seems that the more comfortable situations tend to produce apathetic work, whereas in the more uncomfortable ones we tend to produce our best paintings and our best art and our best dramas and our best cars and our best synthesizers. So being uncomfortable isn't such a bad thing.

TS: What does *satyagraha* [name of a Glass opera] mean?

PG: *Satyagraha* is Gandhi's word for his activist, non-violent movement, and it means literally "truth force." He didn't like passive resistance. He thought that word didn't suggest the active nature of the movement. This movement began in South Africa in 1893. He was there from 1893 to 1914, and that's where he developed his political skills. He went there when he was twenty one and he left when he was forty three. This opera is about those years, how Gandhi created the personality and the political force that was Gandhi.

TS: Martin Bernheimer of the *Los Angeles Times* did a scathing critique of your concert here. When you read a review like that, how do you react to it?

PG: I never read it. I'm not particularly interested in reviews. The good ones are never good enough, and the bad ones just waste my time. I get angry and I discover I'm thinking of replies to make to people. I stopped reading reviews years ago. I've heard about that particular review. It's much quoted.

TS: This guy won a Pulitzer Prize.

PG: What I heard sounded very silly, and maybe because I didn't read it I might not be being fair to it. Maybe it wasn't as silly as what I heard. But to tell you the truth, being part of a controversy is a lot of fun. I don't know if people like that realize how supportive they are in a certain way. It continues the discussion. I feel the music is not at all controversial. I think these kinds of controversies are tempest-in-the-teapot deals. What I see is that people love the music.

TS: Are you a Buddhist?

PG: I keep reading about that in the paper. I also read in the paper that I was born in Chicago, which I was not. I was born in Baltimore. But in fact I have a lot of friends in the Buddhist community, especially the Tibetan community when it came out of Tibet and came over to the States. Seminars and study groups were started. In the early days, in order for funding, to get the money to start these centers, I did a concert every year for the Tibet Center in New York. I did a concert last summer for a retreat center in Canada, organized by the Naropa Institute. And I have really good friends, both Tibetan and American, in those communities. So I do whatever I can for it. I think it's a real interesting, important cultural ingredient that's become part of our lives.

TS: Do you look back on your formal studies with Nadia Boulanger [renowned French music teacher] as relics from a past age of European composition?

PG: Oh, no, no, no. There's no way I could write the music I write today without having studied with that particular person. In fact when young people ask me what they should study, they don't like what I tell them because I tell them a lot of counterpoint, a lot of analysis. See, I write with pencil and paper. Maybe I'm the dinosaur. A lot of people don't work that way any more.

TS: The ensemble you perform with has remained an extraordinarily tight group. How long have you been together?

PG: Almost twenty years, and it's allowed us to reach a level of performance I couldn't have done otherwise. You have to remember, we've played some of these pieces two hundred times. So after about sixty or eighty times they really start rolling along.

TS: Are there any particular artists in other media that you have an affinity towards?

PG: Oh, many, in the theater arts and individual arts. I worked with Richard Serra for a long time. I was his studio assistant for about three years. He's a sculptor who at the moment is very controversial because of his big public pieces. There are some movements in different cities to take his pieces down. But when I began with the ensemble it was the artists like Richard Serra or Don Judd or Sol LeWitt, Bob Rauschenberg, Jasper Johns, who helped me build equipment, provided places for me to play. So I really came out of that world of the visual arts. And then I have active collaborative relationships with people in the theater arts, like Bob Wilson

and the Mabou Mines.
TS: Didn't I see a painting of you at the Whitney Museum?
PG: Yeah, Chuck Close did what they used to call photo-realist—it was never really that—but he did portraits based on photographs. And there's a picture—it's kind of my Dorian Gray photo—of me in 1968, and I looked ten years older than the picture at the time. Now I look about the same age as the person in the picture.

1985

JOE JACKSON

Though Joe Jackson is best known as a rock artist, I became a fan of his in 1981 with Jumpin Jive, *an album based on early R&B and jazz tunes. Late that year I saw him whip a Newcastle, England music hall crowd into a jitterbug frenzy. A few years later he was writing political songs; his next album was instrumental, with orchestral passages reminiscent of Delius and Vaughan Williams. Why all these sudden changes of direction? I knew I wanted to pin him down about it. During our conversation he spoke openly about this and other issues.*

TS: Do you think your new instrumental LP, *Will Power,* will come as a surprise to your fans?

JJ: Well, you'd have to ask them, really. I don't know. I don't even know who they are. I think it's probably a varied bunch of people that changes somewhat from one record to the next. It probably does come as a surprise, because not many people make instrumental records in the rock or pop field.

TS: It certainly isn't the cheapest way of making a record.

JJ: Well, that depends how you look at it. Only about three

STOLEN MOMENTS

*"If you want to make
genuine major changes in society,
then playing a guitar and singing
isn't the way to do it . . ."*

weeks of studio time went into making it. Billy Idol just spent $1.5 million making his latest record. I could make twenty records for that.

TS: Well, you've always liked that idea of going into the studio with a band and doing it as live as possible.

JJ: Definitely. I believe in the honest approach.

TS: Why did you call the new album *Will Power?*

JJ: The piece on the album called "Will Power" was untitled for about two years. I could never think of a title for it. It's very difficult to get a title for an instrumental piece, because you're not necessarily telling a literal story. But sometimes you try to communicate a certain feeling. And with that piece it's a feeling of determination—with a hint of desperation or something. *Will Power* seemed to me a pretty good title since the whole project was held together by nothing much else.

TS: The first piece on the album is called "*No Pasaran.*" Why did you use the Spanish Civil War slogan?

JJ: Well, it may have been a Spanish Civil War slogan, but it's the Sandinista slogan now. And I used that because I wanted to try to tell a story of what's been happening in Nicaragua, which is something that I feel very strongly about and very angry about—U.S. policy towards Nicaragua. The piece has a build-up of tension and violence, which then kind of explodes into revolution, then dies down again into a continuing violence. The piece ends ambiguously, to suggest that the tension's continuing, and we don't know quite where it's going to go. I try to tell that story in a very direct emotional way rather than clutter it up with words. I don't know if there would have been a way of writing a song about it and saying it in words without sounding preachy or clumsy. I would think this is the most direct way to say how I feel.

TS: Are there pressures to remain a pop artist once you're a pop artist and not do records like this?

JJ: Well, I think that in these circumstances a lot of artists put pressure on themselves. But you know, a lot of people, once they have a little bit of success, get their priorities mixed up.

They become a bit too concerned with being secure, or they become motivated by a fear of not being as rich and famous as they think they deserve to be. Or they've grown accustomed to a certain lifestyle and they find themselves owing a lot of money to their record company. I think the artist in the long run is responsible. No one can force you to go in to a studio and make a particular kind of record, but people do allow themselves to be pressured.

TS: Are you a restless artist?

JJ: In some ways. I'm always looking for ways to make the music challenging, fresh. But what's more important is I'm always trying to maintain a certain quality. I don't put anything out unless I really believe in it. Everybody always tells me that I change styles all the time, right?

TS: That's pretty obvious.

JJ: Which I don't really agree with.

TS: No?

JJ: No. I think people tend to oversimplify things to make it easier to talk about certain artists. If you just look at what I've done in a superficial way, then it might seem this way. I mean, I keep hearing that my *Night And Day* album was a concept album about life in New York, which it wasn't. But somehow that's got into people's heads and it becomes a cliché that's repeated. My first two albums were new wave rock and roll, then *Jumpin Jive* was a jazz album, and then I did a Latin album. If you look at it a bit more closely it's always been eclectic right from the start. I just think that I've shown different sides of what I've been able to do on different records. And it takes more that one or two records to say everything I've wanted to say.

TS: Do you think that music can change or affect the world?

JJ: Not really. I think it's a little naive to think so, in terms of changing a political situation or helping feed the starving millions. That's not what music was designed to do. I think sometimes lyrics can help to make people think or raise their consciousness a bit. But a lot of the time that's not going to happen if you're preaching to the converted in the first place. If you say anything within a rock-pop context, you're basically addressing an audience inclined to have similar opinions.

TS: The politicians don't have much time to listen to music.

JJ: No, which is probably one of the reasons why they're in the state they're in. But I do think music is intended to be a communication between people, to share ideas and emotions. I think it can enrich the quality of people's lives and contribute to people using their brains to do what brains were designed to do, which is to think and be aware of what's going on in the world and be aware of each other. It goes beyond just facile entertainment. But I think if you want to make genuine major changes in society, then playing a guitar and singing isn't the way to do it. I wish more people would be a little more realistic about that.

1987

KEITH JARRETT

KEITH JARRETT IS FOR ME A MUSICAL PARADIGM: SEATED IN *front of the big Steinway with his sneakers and teeshirt on, waiting for the muse to enter, then improvising impossibly beautiful melodies and harmonies for a solid hour. He has it all: technique, dynamics, harmonic sense, a gutsy blues feel.*

I went to the airport in a borrowed Cadillac to pick him up along with his drummer, Jack DeJohnette, wondering what type of music should be coming out of the great Delco sound system that General Motors puts into its cars. I decided to leave it on our station, KCRW; its West African rhythms wafted through the interior of the land yacht. Jarrett gave the radio a disgusted look, then reached for the knob and turned it off without saying a word.

He was at once very precise, almost Zen-like, in his use of language, yet his meanings were often opaque and mysterious, at least to my ears. After thirty minutes he hadn't acknowledged my presence except as the chauffeur.

We got to the station and went into the studio. When the interview was over a half-hour later, I wasn't sure that I knew any more about him than before. Yet few pianists have touched me as deeply as he has, and I knew this book would be incomplete without him.

TS: How did you get involved in music in the beginning? Were you pushed or did you jump?

KJ: I jumped, but I have to believe what I was told because I was too young to remember. But at three years old, I don't think I would have been pushed.

TS: Were your parents interested in music?

KJ: No, they weren't. They discovered that I had perfect pitch eventually, because there was an old piano and I was able to play along with some stuff on the radio.

TS: Did you think or dream of music? Did it have some sort of fascination for you?

KJ: No. From then to now I don't think I can say it was ever a dream of any kind. It was manifest, but it wasn't a dream.

TS: When did it start becoming more real for you? When did you start playing more and listening more?

KJ: Well, I don't know. I guess in my mid-teens. By that time I had played long enough that I could deal with the instrument well for my age. Not as well as I can now, but I think that's one of the best things about starting early. When you start to finally have ideas or are curious about what you might do, if you don't have the ability to deal with some of the ideas you have, it's more frustrating than anything. Most musicians, including probably myself, might not get past that point.

TS: When you did *The Köln Concert* it was a groundbreaking new LP. People hadn't heard anything like it before. Did you know that the LP would be so successful?

KJ: I've never known that anything would be successful, but Manfred [Eicher, ECM producer] and I have always shared a knowledge of how good we felt something was. When we did the Köln concert, first of all, everything was against it being good. It was the wrong piano that had been rented, it was out of adjustment completely, it was the wrong brand of piano, we hadn't slept for two days, and the engineers were almost told to leave and go back home. We said, "Well, we might as well record it while they're here and we'll keep a copy of whatever happens." So then we listened to it in the car and we both silently stared at each other now and then, knowing that we had to somehow release it because of how good it was.

TS: Do you resent all the other solo pianists that have . . .

KJ: How can I say I resent? Do you have more of the question? I have a feeling I know what you mean.

TS: Yes. George Winston and the hordes that followed him.

KJ: I don't think I can resent something that is unconscious. I would say I am saddened a little but I don't think I can say I resent it. How can I resent something that exists with its own set of experiences and its own limits when I know very well everything has limits?

TS: Were the solo piano tours exhausting?

KJ: Oh, yes, definitely. More exhausting than any other. I'm saying this now because I've tried a couple of times to think of what to compare a solo tour to, and the only thing I can compare it to is an athlete on a very, very tightly scheduled tour of marathons. And yet, since it wasn't billed as that, and I was not considered an athlete, I was setting up tours that were possible to do with a certain amount of energy, but had never been attempted with the amount of energy that I needed for what I was doing. In other words, there might be twenty concerts in a month and that would be normal for a recitalist, but for me, I never knew just how much energy there really was.

TS: For every musician there must be times when he or she will get to the concert hall and just say, "God! I just don't feel like playing tonight. I feel terrible, I ate something that didn't agree with me, I'm depressed, I'm down . . ." For you, in your solo concerts, were there days where it was difficult to get up there?

KJ: From sickness, yes. But even then, the psychological thing you're describing didn't exist. Because I was always more curious about what might happen under the new given situation than I was depressed about having to attempt it.

TS: Will you ever tour solo again?

KJ: I don't know. It seems to be separate from me. It was not something that I consciously invented. I didn't just sit at home and decide one day that the appropriate thing for me to do would be to go out and play alone with no material. It came to me as I was doing other things that were considered normal, and it became what I did, and it stopped, in a way, and I have no control over whether it will be done in the future or not until I start doing it.

TS: One thing I've noticed about you is that you can seem to be very deep inside yourself and what you're doing, and yet be acutely aware of what's going on around you. For example, when the phone rings offstage, you stop playing and say, "Will someone please answer the phone?", or an evening when you weren't finished and people started applauding, and you sort of shook your head and walked off stage, and I said to myself, "Oh, no, it's stopping now, it broke the spell." Is that what happens?

KJ: That's what happens for the listener. What happens for me is that there's a process going on and, since it's an open process by virtue of there not being any material, anything can change it, any accidental thing can alter its course, and so you just saw that. But if my ears are supposed to be open for what comes next, then certainly the telephone is going to play a part in that. But your description of my being aware, of being deeply inside and also aware of normal goings-on, should apply to an artist of any kind. Otherwise, what's he doing? I mean, he's bringing something to a world that he has to be sensitive to in order to make it a gift to that world.

TS: You toured all over the world—Europe, Japan, of course the States. Do you prefer a certain audience for a particular reason, in terms of silence, in terms of . . .

KJ: Well, each of those terms has a part of the world that I could say "yes" to. Silence: Japan. There are aggressive and exciting audiences. For example, when I go to play Japan, not nearly as much pressure is put upon music to be anything in particular. And even if there is that pressure, they don't give it away. They're too polite to tell you what they want you to do. So whenever I've had any bands or been there alone, I've realized a kind of freedom that's not possible in other places where audiences are really up for this event and have their ways of showing it.

TS: What's the experiential difference between playing a solo improvised concert, classical written music, and improvising with a group?

KJ: I could say many things about that question. I said one thing yesterday about the difference between solo improvising and group playing tunes, which was, "How can you compare nothing to something?" But there's more, because now that you're adding the classical thing, it leads me to be able to describe all three things as being one thing. There's nothing—if you call it nothing—in solo concerts. Nothing exists except a process, and in the process something might exist of substance, and it might not.

Then there's tunes that the trio plays which are substantial, but which can be blown away by the merest little breeze if that's where the music goes, or can stay fairly substantially noticeable. And then there's written music, which is substance without changeability except for the intensity of the interpretation. If you put all those things together, that's music. In a solo concert sometimes it becomes so substantial that it is a written piece.

That's why a lot of people think the Köln concert was conceived before it was played. And with the best of classical interpreters, you get the sense that you're hearing the piece for the first time. So even though it's substantial, it's suddenly born. And then, with the trio, to me the most interesting thing is that if people play together who are conscious of those other two modes of expression, they can bring a new design over it without erasing the concept.

TS: Is there any one of those three where you're most vulnerable, if indeed you feel vulnerable at all?

KJ: If I don't feel vulnerable, I'm not doing my job. My job is to be open to the possibilities of the music, even in Bartok. But the most vulnerable, by far, is certainly with the least material, so that a solo concert is the most vulnerable of all those things.

TS: Do you listen to your own albums?

KJ: Yes, but you know, in the process of making an album I have to hear those albums quite a bit, and I'm not one of those guys who goes around and wants to hear the tapes the day before the next concert. We make documentary recordings when we do concerts, and even though I can listen to them, I usually don't until I've got a long space of time. So it wouldn't influence what I played tonight if I listened to last night's.

TS: If you had to name two people, as some of the greatest people in playing classical music in the last thirty years, does anybody come to mind?

KJ: You're talking about classical players? Or people that I would say I would like to . . . ?

TS: Anybody. Art Tatum. Glenn Gould.

KJ: I wonder why we need names here. Okay, Glenn Gould and Bud Powell. How about that? Not necessarily in that order.

TS: Did you ever play a live concert that reached a sort of perfect moment, or some sort of perfection that you've searched for?

KJ: If you search for something and never find it. But I think I know what you mean anyway. Yes, in fact it's recorded, on the *Concerts* album, which is the last thing so far that's been released by me on solo piano, the end of . . . I'm not sure whether it's Bregenz or Munich—I think it's Munich. At the end of the Munich concert there's a thing that started to happen in the strings, and I'm just playing the strings as I have done in the past. And it was even visible to the friends of mine who were there in the audience, that I had left the stage, and all that was left on the stage was this thing that was happening, and it was like I was subsidiary to this thing. There's an example of being where I had to be. That's where it all happens.

TS: Are you an idealist?

KJ: I don't know. If you define the word I'll tell you. That's a word that's used an awful lot. What do you mean?

TS: Are there certain things that you aspire to that you maybe don't find in the daily run of events, an ideal of beauty, things that you search for to give life more meaning, that take you out of the depressing things that you read in the newspapers?

KJ: Well, I'm not an idealist in the sense that I think that we don't need those depressing things somehow. I mean, I don't believe that I'm living in an illusion and I'm looking for reality. But I believe that reality is so much more than what we normally think it is, that there have to be consciously made efforts toward remembering, at least, what all the reality is at any time, instead of accepting this depressing world we live in as being reality. Not that it isn't reality, but within it is always the seed of remembering what it's all about, so that if you could get to it, you'd be at a place where all these depressing things would be a necessary part of all the non-depressing things. So as an artist I'm an idealist, because in my art I try to show what more there is.

TS: Are there any art forms that move or affect you in a similar way as music? Any writers, painters or poets?

KJ: Writers, poets . . . I live in a world of sound, so writers and poets are much more effective to me. The death of Italo Calvino was a very shocking thing to me. Almost as shocking as Glenn Gould. Writers, I can hear their sound. And poets. I think artists, if they can appreciate something outside their art, it's great, but if they can't it doesn't mean anything. They might be so involved in their thing that they just can't see it all.

1985

"If [my work] and my public life has given the Maori people somebody to look up to, that's what I'd be very proud of...."

KIRI TE KANAWA

KIRI TE KANAWA'S MAGNIFICENT SOPRANO IS A VOICE TO LEVItate by. *Her singing is matched by her sensual beauty and poise on stage. Born in New Zealand to a Maori tribesman father and an Irish mother, she's the antithesis of a haughty diva off-stage, a devoted mother and down-to-earth woman who wears bluejeans and would rather drive a truck than a car.*

TS: What do you like most about singing?

KK: I think that people aren't often given the opportunity to participate in something they enjoy that much. I like to listen to music, but also to be able to sing it, to take part in it, is a great thrill.

TS: If you had an instrument to play other than your voice, what might it be?

KK: Well, there are three instruments I find very beautiful—the French horn, the flute and the oboe.

TS: What are the negative sides of being an internationally famous diva?

KK: I suppose there are quite a lot. You are separated from your family, places that you like, and people that you like. Quite often you don't really make many friends around the world. You can't keep up the friendship.

TS: What have been your favorite operatic roles?

KK: If they all weren't my favorite roles I wouldn't enjoy what I'm doing. You have to sing and take part in things you really love. Every role I do I love. But in particular, I enjoy doing Arabella, or the Countess in *Figaro*, or Elvira in *Don Giovanni*.

TS: Do you have a most treasured performance?

KK: I suppose there are quite a few of them. My very first Countess at Covent Garden, which started me on an international career, really, in a big way. And Desdemona in *Otello* at the Met. Some performances I've been sad to step away from, thinking it's a lovely cast, a nice situation.

TS: Do you have particular divas you've admired the most?

KK: When I was starting out I used to love to listen to Leontyne Price. Now whenever I get the opportunity I like to see her. I love male singers—Pavarotti and Domingo.

TS: How do you protect yourself from burnout?

KK: Good question. I don't socialize. If you don't socialize, you don't party and do dinners and cocktail parties, if you can avoid all of that, you tend to be able to look after the job at hand.

TS: Has it ever happened that you blanked out while singing an opera?

KK: No, because in opera you always have a prompter. But I did have a terrific dream the other day. I've been at the Met over the last two months. I sang "Fiudilici" in *Cosi Fan Tutti*. On the last night, after I had finished my very last performance, I went to sleep. I woke up the next morning, and discovered that I had had a nightmare that I had never finished the performance! It was four o'clock in the morning, Jimmy Levine was still conducting, I was still singing, and I had several more arias and duets and whatever to go. And I never, ever finished the opera. I woke up at nine o'clock the next morning having never completed the opera, it was so long!

TS: Is there one country or particular audience who gets the most emotional in opera? Would it be an Italian audience, men who prostrate themselves at your feet at the end of a performance?

KK: Yes, these things happen. I suppose if you put them all into one bunch you'd think gosh, this is too much. But you get a very demonstrative audience in Paris. They want to tell you how to sing it, and if they don't like you they tell you, and if they do like you they do tell you. If they hate the conductor he's booed off the stage. When I was in Paris for a few years it was quite frightening, wondering who was going to get booed off the stage tonight. That was, I think, the most vocal audience.

TS: What goes into a voice? Are some people born with great voices?

KK: Yes, I do believe that now, although I heard a very great tenor sing once, and he didn't have half the voice of his father. I know my father had a very beautiful voice. With my own children I really don't know what they will have.

TS: Is there any one thing in your career that you're most proud of?

KK: I think, if I look back, that I'm very proud of the nation I was born in. It's a little country with a very little-known race of people, the Maori people. And whatever my work and my public life has done, if it's given them somebody to look up to, that's what I'd be very proud of, that they could follow somebody who didn't do any man any harm, and improved herself and pulled herself up by her coattails and did something with a life that could have been a mess.

TS: There is an indigenous Maori music, is there not?

KK: Yes, it's a primitive sort of music. It's more chanting, akin to the American Indian music in some ways. I think if one did a deep search into both those cultures you'd find a large similarity.

TS: One thing that struck me upon reading about you and meeting you is that you don't seem like a diva. You seem approachable, a very normal-type person. Do you get that reaction much?

KK: (laughs) Yes, I do. I'm not a very good liar, and I can't live an untruth. So I find it much easier to be me, and natural and truthful. Sometimes it doesn't always work, but in most cases it keeps me happy, keeps my feet on the ground. Somebody wrote to me and said, "How can you call your profession a job?" And I thought to myself, how am I ever going to say to my children, "I'm off to do my profession today"? Or, "I'm at my profession." I find it very difficult to use large words for something that's very simple. A job is a job. I do a job. It just seems to be out of other people's hours. I work nights where other people work days.

1988

MIRIAM MAKEBA

LONG BEFORE THE NEW WAVE OF AFRICAN ARTISTS LIKE KING
*Sunny Ade and Ladysmith Black Mambazo, long before Sun
City and the media focus on South Africa, there was Miriam
Makeba, the first African artist to become popular in America. Her
voice captivated listeners with its simplicity and elegance, its clicks
and vocal nuances. Her early albums drew attention to the richness
of Bantu, Zulu, and Kwela musical culture.*

*Forced into exile after leaving South Africa, the doors of her
homeland have remained shut to her. But her performances with
Paul Simon and a newly published autobiography have brought her
to the attention of a new generation of Americans. Our conversation was rich, and revealing.*

TS: What prompted you to write your autobiography, Miriam?
MM: I was talked into doing it by a friend from South Africa. She came to Guinea five years ago and said, "You ought to write about your life." I said, "What is there to write?" She said, "You don't understand. You're the first to leave our country and make an impact outside. We would like to know what

STOLEN MOMENTS

*"When you are suddenly booted
from your own surroundings and told
that you can't go home,
you are just completely deranged..."*

your road has been like." Now it's finished, out there giving me a lot of trouble. (laughs)

TS: Has it been difficult for you as the most popular South African singer in the world, and, as one of the first, to maintain a private life?

MM: I had a private life until I wrote this book. A lot of people were surprised that I've been married five times. They never knew that because I never talked about my life in public. There were things that I never said to anyone, even those who feel they are close to me. Some of them were surprised seeing some of the things I said. The only problem I have had is having to carry a lot of Africa on my shoulders, They say, "You're African. Tell us this." Some people call me spokesman, which I don't think I am because I can't speak for anybody. I just speak because I have experienced that kind of life myself, you see. But sometimes people want to interview me about my singing and we end up talking about South Africa. That has been a strain.

TS: What was the most difficult thing about writing this book for you?

MM: Just talking about certain private things. Most of all, talking about my child was not very easy, because it was still very fresh. She had just died. I still find it difficult.

TS: What are your earliest memories?

MM: I remember very little of my father because he died when I was small. I remember, though, very vividly where we lived when he died—my little dog, a lady who was killed by a cat, which makes me afraid of cats today. I remember my school days when I was singing with my little group, my teacher who made me like music and formed the little group for us. And I remember when we had to stand in the rain, supposedly to sing for King George the Fifth, who came and just zoomed through. We caught a glimpse of him, but I don't think he saw or heard us.

TS: You thought you would be discovered then?

MM: We were to perform for him, but the motorcade just passed us by.

TS: Wasn't it the a result of a film you made that you had your first international success?

MM: Yes, *Come Back Africa*. It was filmed at home, in secret. Why, I didn't know. I was asked to sing two songs. A gentleman from New York came to South Africa and stayed a year to make this film. He wrote to me in 1957 that Steve Allen wanted me to appear on his program. I did not believe that. I didn't know who these people were, but just the thought of coming to America . . .

So I applied for a passport. It took me two years to get one, because they had to investigate me, to see if I was with the Communist Party. One time I was coming from the hospital, my first operation. They asked me a lot of questions. "Do you belong to the Communist Party?" I said, "I'm not a Russian." To me that was a very honest answer, because I sincerely thought communists were Russian. I didn't know what it meant until much later. And so I guess they just said, "That one, just give her a passport."

I left to go and represent *Come Back Africa,* which had been entered in the Venice Film Festival in 1959. It won the Critics' Award. Then I went back through France to England where I waited for a visa to come to the United States. While there I met Mr. Belafonte.

TS: One of your first big brothers, right?

MM: Yes. Mr. Belafonte came to see *Come Back Africa* the following day, and he said, "I like your work very much." So I told him I was going to come here to do the Steve Allen Show, and he said, "When you come if there's anything you need, here's my phone number." I finally got the visa and came. I had nothing—no written music, no musicians. Mr. Belafonte started to get together all of those things for me, and within three days I rehearsed and came to Burbank here to do the Steve Allen Show. I came, I sang, and I left the same night for New York to open at the Vanguard. What was to be four weeks became ten years.

TS: What were your impressions? Wasn't it overwhelming to be driven around in limousines and have the star treatment here?

MM: Oh, that started in England and in Venice. I said, "What is this?" I was very frightened because I had no training in that. At home the only normal relationship we have with whites is that of master and servant. I was not used to socializing with white people. So it was very uncomfortable for me from the time I boarded the plane in Johannesburg to go to London. I was the only black person on the plane and I felt terrible. I sat like a frightened cat in a corner.

And in London, while I was waiting for this visa, I used to walk around and feel very hungry. I would look into a restaurant and see white people sitting there and just know I couldn't go in there. After 27 years of my life, that's in the head. I'd see policemen and shiver because I thought, "Well these men, even though they are supposed to protect, they often abuse." So it took me a long time to understand that I was not in South Africa, and that I could sit and talk to white people without being frightened.

TS: Leaving South Africa when you did, did you have any idea that you would be going into exile, in effect?

MM: No. If I did, I probably would not have left. I was supposed to be abroad only four weeks. After my performances on Steve Allen and at the Village Vanguard, I was fortunate that all the reviews were so favorable that I started getting calls to do the universities. So it just kept extending. Finally my mother said, "Send for your child." So I sent for my daughter and she came. I stayed, and then I found out when my mother died that I couldn't go home. That was a big shock because I did not expect that.

TS: Why couldn't you go home?

MM: I wish I knew. Why does the South African government do anything? Why do they arrest little children and torture them? Why do they throw tear gas on babies? Why can't we vote? Why can't we live where we live? Why did they have to have the Immorality Act? Why do they have the Group Areas Act? It boils down to one thing, racism. And a superiority complex.

TS: What's been the most difficult part of being in exile for you?

MM: When you are suddenly booted from your own surroundings and told that you can't go there, you are just completely deranged. I could say, "I know. I'll take the plane and go home tomorrow." But you know that even when you have that feeling, all of a sudden, "Hey, I can't go." It's enough to drive one crazy. Everything about being in exile is difficult. Most of the time people are kind, but there are times when they let you know that you are with them but not of them.

TS: Do you think that the situation in South Africa will get worse before it gets better?

MM: I don't know. But it is worse right now. People say it's changing, but I say, "Where is it changing?" If it's changing, why do they need to have a state of emergency imposed? Why do they have to keep men and women of the press out? If it had changed for the better there would be no need for creating a bureau of information that chops up the news, takes out what they want, leaves out what they don't want to be said.

TS: Do you think there's a solution?

MM: I don't know. If I had the solution I would wave that magic wand right now and go home the next minute, I swear. The South African government talks about violence. Well, they're the most violent people I have ever known. They talk about terrorism. They are the number one terrorists in the world. And they expect us to always turn the other cheek. People say the ANC is violent. Who's violent, you know? The violence comes from the government side. Even the fact that we go hungry and we have nowhere to live in a country as rich as South Africa—that's violent.

TS: I want to talk a little bit about music.

MM: Thank you. (sighs)

TS: First of all I want to congratulate you on your new album *Sangoma.* Your mother was an *asangoma,* a healer. And she taught you these songs.

MM: Most of them.

TS: Why did you decide to do an album of healing songs?

MM: Russ Titelman, my producer, came to me and sang in my ear a song that I recorded some years ago without any music. I just inserted that song in a whole album that had all the instruments, and he singled out that song. I turned around, and he said, "I'm Russ Titelman, a record producer." I said, "Where did you hear that song?" He said, "I heard that song and I love it. I'd like to make an album with you of such songs. Do you have any more?" I said, "There's many where that came from." He said, "I'd really like that." I did not believe him.

We left, we went to Europe, Australia, and on the last leg of the tour with Paul Simon he called again. He said, "I still want to make that album." So we arranged to make a demonstration tape singing the songs. Then I said to myself, "Why not those songs?" So I sang the traditional healer's songs, and he liked the tape. We went in the studio and recorded it. I think it's for him that this album was made, because can you imagine me going to any big company and telling them I want to make an album of this kind?

TS: Do you think often of your mother?

MM: Always. I never saw my mother dead. For a long time I used to talk of my mother as if she were still alive. I'd say, "My mother is" instead of "my mother was." Maybe it's because I didn't see her dead. My image of her is the one when I left and she was very much alive.

TS: Do you have a fondest memory of her, a particular one that you cherish?

MM: Yes, I can't talk about that one. (laughs) It's something I used to do for her when she was not in a good mood, she was down. I would take off all of my clothes for her and she would laugh and laugh (laughs) and tell me to get out of the room.

TS: What exactly is a healing song? Is it a song someone sings to you when you're sick?

MM: No. When they have to concentrate to be able to find out what is ailing you and what they can use to cure you, there are certain songs that we sing which are very quiet songs to help them to concentrate. They are sung by a traditional medical person, just like a doctor, but I wouldn't dare call them a doctor because I would be asked which university did they go to. They call them witch doctors here. (laughs) You can't be a doctor and a witch at the same time. Doctors

cure, witches make magic.
- *TS:* Music for you has always been a spiritual force, hasn't it?
- *MM:* I like to sing. I'm happy when I sing, even when I sing a sad song. Inside I am happy.
- *TS:* Do you think that music brings people closer to a—you use the phrase "superior being?"
- *MM:* Somebody, something created all of us. Call him God or whatever. There is someone somewhere, something. There should be a reason why we're all here, I think, I believe. So he is called so many names. I was brought up a little Christian, so I would say God.
- *TS:* This is a big question. If you had your life to live over again are there certain things you'd do differently?
- *MM:* Well, I certainly wouldn't want the downs. I would want my whole to life to be beautiful ups. (laughs) I've had too many downs. I would really want to avoid those.

1988

BRANFORD MARSALIS

WE WERE TO HAVE BEGUN OUR CONVERSATION AT 11 A.M. At 11:15 I called him at the hotel. "House of Grief," the voice answered. I told him to put his rear in gear: fifteen minutes later, there he was, with a big smile and a hug.

It was only a few years ago that Branford Marsalis emerged from his younger brother Wynton's shadow. If Wynton is one of the best classical trumpeters in the world, Branford certainly ranks among the elite of jazz saxophonists. More listeners, though, have probably seen or heard him through his work with rock idol Sting. Branford Marsalis is an open person, a philosopher of life—articulate, street smart, and funny.

TS: Branford, what makes music special to you as opposed to the other arts?

BM: What makes jazz music more special than any other thing is that it is the only art form that is actually conceived in the present tense. When you see a truly great work of art, like a Rembrandt, a Monet, or a Van Gogh, I think it's similar. But I don't think art can soothe you the way that music can. I can't

"There's a big difference between people who make music and people who [just] play music..."

give you a physical explanation as to why, but I'm much more comforted by things that I associate with my ear than things that I associate with my eye. I think another thing that makes music special is that it's heard, and not seen or touched or anything else.

TS: Do you get sick of being a musician?

BM: Definitely. That's the musician's curse. I can't live up to my own expectations. Nothing you do is ever good enough. It's very frustrating after a while. I could see myself doing another job, but it would have to be something just as challenging, something to do with my imagination, like computer programming or engineering. You know, radio deejay, something like that. (laughs) I don't think I have the temperament for a regular job, where you have to do the same thing all the time. It has to be something where you have the ability to create things, or to shift and change directions. I think I'll always come back to music, though, in the long run.

When we finished the tour and the record, I came home and put my horn in the case and pushed it in the closet for three and a half weeks. I didn't look at it, I didn't think about it. I sanded and polyurethaned floors in my house, got some spackling done on the ceiling, got some guys in to repair the ceiling and build the porch. I played with my kid, went to Virginia, enjoyed my family. And now I'm going crazy. It's time to start playing music again. I think I need to do that, have an off season to give me the desire.

TS: Do you like being famous? You are relatively well known now.

BM: Well, if this is fame, I like this. I like it when you come through customs and the guy looks and he says, "Branford Marsalis. Do you work with him?" And I say, "Yeah, I do." And he says, "Well, where is he?" And I say, "You're looking at him." And he looks at me, he looks around me, and he says, "Where? Where is he?" And I say, "I'm him," and he says, "You ain't him!" I like that. I can rent a car and not really be hassled. I can drive where I want to go, and go to concerts and football games. I don't need the other thing—people constantly grabbing you, stopping you in the phone booth, in the bathroom. The thing I like most about my position now is the respect I get from my peers, which is much more important to me than the press saying, "Hey, he knows what's happening!"

TS: How did this thing with Sting happen? Were you aware of his music before you guys met?

BM: When you spend an amount of time practicing your instrument and doing musical research, you can tell which guys do their homework. If you listen to a symphonic performer, a classical soloist, you can tell the difference between a guy who has studied the music, read the books, and done the research on the composer and listened to all the different variations of pieces as he was growing up—and the guy who just sat down and learned all the right notes, got it down fast and technical, and plays it in his songs like glass.

There's a big difference between people who make music and people who play music, especially in pop music now. Most of those guys are just playing music. They're holding their instruments, and the most important thing is what they're wearing. By the first time I heard The Police I had stopped listening seriously to pop music because it was getting so degenerate musically and in every other way.

I was at Berklee College of Music in Boston and a friend of mine said, "Man, you ought to check these guys out." This was in 1980. I was really impressed by the quality of the music, the melodic content as it worked against the rhythmic counterparts. There were contrapuntal lines in pop music again. It was a shock at first.

TS: So it was the musicianship as well as the lyrics?

BM: The lyrics, the musicianship, the band concept among all three guys, not just Sting. You felt a great freedom in the music. It wasn't just that drum machine click-track crap that you hear nowadays. Every album got better and better. So I had known about Sting and his work long before they approached me to do the gig.

TS: The people who are screaming for Sting at the concerts probably wouldn't know who you are and they probably wouldn't go buy a jazz album. Am I wrong?

BM: Well, I'd say that twenty percent of the audience can hear the music. The other ones relate to the vibe, the feel, the festive atmosphere.

TS: It's hero worship.

BM: Yeah, but a surprising number of people are actually paying attention to the music, which was a surprise in America, because Americans aren't taught any discipline, to listen to anything.

TS: People get used to entertainment. It breeds laziness.

BM: In Europe it's totally different. Even Canada. One day I was in Canada and I turned on the news, and it dawned on me that there weren't any reports of murders, rapes, killings, because in these times that's not really news. It's that whole syndrome of entertainment. You turn on the FM station—not this one—and it's, *"WXON, YEAHHH, now we have this new hit, bluhbluhbluh..."* It's nothing to do with anything, so how can you expect serious pop musicians or artists any more? They're "music personalities." They're not interested in being musicians.

So you've got a guy like Sting who takes his music very seriously, but how can you expect anybody in the audience to take his music seriously? I feel sorry for him. He's in a Catch-22 situation. But I admire him. He decided he wanted to go solo and when he did he borrowed from every example of music he thought was great. And that's the thing that makes his music special.

1987

"Music doesn't recognize any frontier, any language or... political differences. It speaks directly from person to person..."

JOHN McLAUGHLIN

IT IS NOT UNCOMMON TO SEE ENRAPTURED YOUNG GUITARISTS AT *John McLaughlin concerts with small recorders hidden in their jackets—a measure of his tremendous influence among guitar players. His Mahavishnu Orchestra, and later Shakti, were among the most important fusion groups of the 1970's, though I had first heard him on Miles Davis' album* In a Silent Way.

John McLaughlin is tall, debonair, strikingly handsome. He walked into the studio relaxed and smiling, smoking a cigarette. It didn't surprise me that after he mentioned on the air that he enjoyed playing tennis and swimming, several women called asking him if he was free that afternoon to play a set or swim some laps.

TS: How did you get started in music, John?

JM: My mom was an amateur violinist, so that was a big encouragement. I grew up without TV for the first eight years in a tiny village with a name nobody knows. It's not even a dot on the map. Then we moved to an even smaller town called Whitley Bay, which is near the boundary between England and Scotland. From the beginning there was always music on the radio, predominantly classical. By the time the blues boom had started in England many years ago my brothers were in college, and they brought it home on records.

This movement grew in popularity to the Rolling Stones, who of course took their names from one of Muddy Waters' songs. And the rock and roll movement stemmed from this. But rhythm and blues was very popular in the early sixties, which was close to jazz. Of course the sophistication and elegance and eloquence that Miles Davis developed through his own group, and subsequently other musicians, played an important part for me. But that raw blues feeling was there.

TS: Most Americans first heard you on Miles Davis' *In A Silent Way*.

JM: Of course to be able to play with Miles was wonderful, a dream.

TS: How did that come about?

JM: One day the drummer Jack DeJohnette played Tony Williams, Miles' drummer, a tape that he'd made with Dave Holland and myself in England when he was over there with Bill Evans. Tony was thinking of putting a band together, and said, "I'd like you to come over and do something." So I came over for that. Miles had never heard me, but he knew that I was there to do something with Tony, so he just said, "Come in and bring your guitar."

TS: Was that a little intimidating?

JM: Very! I was shaking. It was "In A Silent Way." Joe Zawinul brought the tune in. It was quite different. We tried it this way and that, and I was nervous, shaking like a leaf. Miles was unhappy with the way it was going. Finally he said, "I want only guitar." And I said, "You want everything? The melody and the chords?" Because usually a guitarist needs time to prepare the inversions to do the melody. Of course he said, "Yes." I said, "That's going to take a little time." He said, "Is that a fact?" That set me off to a really good start.

So he said, "Now why don't you play it like you don't know how to play the guitar?" A typical statement of Miles. I mean, I was already nervous. What does he mean? I had no idea what he was talking about. I was sitting there thinking, "How does a person play who doesn't know how to play?" So I said to myself, "All right, well, he plays with one chord. So play one chord." I played one chord and I started to play the melody, just like that. I didn't know what I was doing. No tempo, just melody and a chord. And I looked around and saw that the engineer had the light on. "Keep going." So I played the melody twice and then Wayne picked it up and them Miles and Wayne played the last thing together. At the end Miles said, "Okay, play it back, Teo." Teo Macero, the producer.

They played it back in the studio and I was in shock, because I saw in a flash what he was going for and how he was able to get something from me that I didn't know I was capable of doing, and from everybody else. He transformed the tune from something that really wasn't working into something of extraordinary beauty.

TS: That project changed a lot of music and certainly was a departure for him.

JM: Miles never stops looking. He's never content to sit on his laurels. Take the group he had in the sixties, with Wayne, Herbie Hancock, Ron Carter, Tony Williams. The conception was so rich that it's going to be valid for a long time to come. But for Miles, by 1969 he was already looking for something else. He constantly searches, and it's a mark of his greatness that he takes risks. There was a guy who came to him in 1969-70 and said, "Why don't you play like you used to?" And Miles said, "How did I used to play?" Of course the guy was saying, "Why don't you play in the format that I know and recognize and feel comfortable with?"

But Miles doesn't do that, and like every great artist he brings everything into question. By doing so I think he constantly renews himself. But of course you run this risk. It's part of the deal.

TS: Did Indian music draw you into your period with Sri Chinmoy? Did the music bring you into that sort of discipline and devotion?

JM: It was actually the other way around. I was a jazz musician who became interested in comparative religion, ways of thought, philosophical and religious. And anybody who gets on that track very quickly finds out that the East is a treasure trove of philosophical and religious thought in general, and India in particular. I was extremely attracted to it. It was so different from the way I was brought up. I thought I could learn a great deal from this thought, which subsequently led me to become a disciple of Sri Chinmoy. The music came as an incidental plus. It was just by accident that I heard Indian music one night many years ago. It escaped me the first time, but that intrigued me. Being a musician, and unable to really grasp what these people were doing, bothered me. It's just music, after all.

But I hung in there and after a short time I "heard" it, and that for me was quite a revelation. I discovered that in fact the Indian musical system, whether it is north or south, is the only other highly organized discipline of improvised music besides jazz. From that point of view we have a tremendous amount in common and we can learn one from the other.

TS: John, tours must be strange when you're playing in a different country every night throughout Europe or Japan. You must get a chance to meet a great variety of people whose common bond is music, and your music in particular.

JM: I'm grateful to be an instrumentalist, because music doesn't recognize any frontier, any language or ideological or political differences. It speaks directly from person to person. It's the social systems that are more or less good. From the point of view of music, I go to Eastern countries, Western countries, it doesn't matter. I meet great people everywhere. What difference is ideology? This is the only way people can deal with each other, by some quirk of human nature—the political solution of going out and beating on somebody's head just because they look different or speak a different language. If we all got together we could solve a lot of problems.

1986

FRANCIS PAUDRAS

HE ASKED ME IF I'D LIKE AN ARMAGNAC AFTER THE SUMPTUOUS *dinner and I said sure. We descended the stone steps into the wine cave. It had an old smell, and what looked like a huge moth was flying back and forth. It turned out to be a bat. He dusted off an old bottle which read "1911." The digestif had been made there by the village priest who had once lived in this house. The cave opened up into a series of tunnels bored out by early Christians escaping Roman persecution.*

We went back upstairs and watched amazing documentary footage from his enormous jazz film archives. Then I turned on a tape recorder, and we began our conversation.

Francis Paudras is an extraordinary man. For him there is no difference between the genius of a Charlie Parker or a Claude Debussy, between Ravel or Bud Powell. Bertrand Tavernier's film Round Midnight *was based upon the unusual friendship of Francis Paudras and the great bebop pianist, Bud Powell. What follows is a glimpse of that remarkable relationship.*

TS: Was *Round Midnight* Bertrand Tavernier's or your idea?

STOLEN MOMENTS

(WITH BUD POWELL)

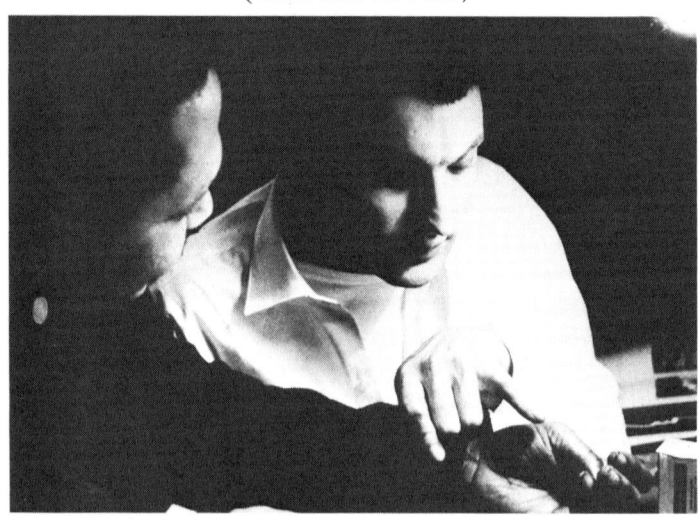

"So here was this genius living on the streets, being put into the hospital or thrown in jail, and people didn't seem to give a damn . . ."

FP: It was Bertrand's. He wanted to make a film about two people with the jazz world as a backdrop, a film about the reuniting of two people. These two characters were originally white—there weren't any blacks in the film's initial conception. Rather, the film was to be a story about people who were exiled for various reasons in France, people whose lives in America had become difficult if not impossible. One of them was a journalist who had left in the wake of McCarthyism. It was a passion for jazz music that brought him together with the other character, a musician. This was Bertrand's initial idea for *Round Midnight*.

One day the critic Alain Gerber told Bertrand that if he wanted documentation of the Paris jazz scene of the late fifties and early sixties—photos, films, etc.—that he should call Francis Paudras. So I got a call from Tavernier saying, "I want to make a film about jazz and I'd like to meet you." He started coming by almost every day and we talked a lot. Bertrand noticed that on the walls at my place there were a lot of photos of musicians, especially Bud Powell, and of Bud and me together. He asked me, "Who is this person?" He didn't know that much about Bud, so I began to tell him about my experiences with him.

After several months he came to me telling me that he had a script ready for me to look over. I stayed up all that night reading it. I was very surprised to see that he had taken my story with Bud almost literally and had used it as the principal story line of the movie. In the background of Tavernier's films there is always the theme of friendship. What interested him about my story with Bud was that it was an unusual, almost impossible friendship based upon the love of jazz music, that brought two separate lives together. One is a musical genius, the other an unknown amateur jazz musician with a regular job, but who is crazy about music. One is black, the other white. They don't speak the same language. It is music that brings them together. The great jazz musician is in distress, while the character based on me simply wishes to give back a little bit of the happiness the musician brought to him all his life with his wonderful music.

TS: When did you first meet Bud Powell?
FP: I must have been about fourteen or fifteen when I first heard Bud, and I was waiting, like many others, for him to come to Paris. He came in 1956 to play at the Salle Pleyel, on the Birdland tour with Miles Davis, Lester Young, and the Modern Jazz Quartet. At that time I was in the military service, but nevertheless I was able to go to the concert. I ran to the concert hall to see this character who for me had become a God, a sort of mythic being. I had a hard time imagining that this person whom I had listened to so much and whose music I loved so much actually existed in flesh and bone.

In 1957, Bud was playing at the Club St. Germain. I didn't miss a night. Like other jazz nuts I got a seat as close to the piano as possible to be able to see Bud's hands while he played. His playing was just out of this world. I was just an amateur jazz pianist, but I wanted to listen to him live and get impregnated with his behavior at the piano. In 1959 we heard that Bud was coming back to Paris to play a new club called the Blue Note. I went by every night, and it was during this period that I began to know Bud a little better. I would go to St. Germain des Près to try to see him. I would walk behind him, watching him. It was fascinating. It was like watching an angel, a sort of extraterrestrial who had landed on this earth.

Later Bud started playing at another club, *Le Chat Qui Pêche,* on the rue de la Huchette. I had no money at the time so I couldn't get into the club, but there was a vent so I could stand next to it and hear the fabulous music coming out. One night while standing there I saw Bud coming out, walking straight towards me. He took me by the hand and asked, "Can you buy me a beer?" I said yes, and took him into the Storyville, a little cafe just across the street.

After a while we left the cafe, with Bud still holding my hand. Ordinarily it would have been somewhat strange to have a grown man holding onto your hand. With Bud it was a natural gesture and a subtle way of communicating. He was so gentle. He held your hand like a small child. He behaved like a child in daily life. So we crossed the street together and walked back into the club. He told the manager that I was his guest. That's how I started getting into the club every night, and discovering him as a human being.

I began to realize that this was a person not like other people. Other people treated him differently too. For instance, the club owners didn't permit him to drink. This interdiction came from Buttercup A. Edwards, who posed as his wife and whom people thought of as such, in spite of Bud's denials, but who in fact was never married to him. At that time she was living with her son and a young musician. She had been asked by Oscar Goodstein, the manager of the New York club Birdland, and also Bud's legal guardian and manager—whose role was played by Martin Scorcese in *Round Midnight*—to be his guardian while he was in Europe and to keep him informed. But she never did. Instead, she exploited him for her own benefit. She decided what Bud would do, how much he would work, and would take all the money he earned.

You couldn't say that Bud was really physically sick, but you couldn't help but notice that he wasn't normal and happy. He seemed just kind of asleep, which could be seen when he was walking. He was forbidden to drink but always wanted to. Each day he'd find somebody to give him a scotch, or money, or he'd just steal somebody's glass from the bar or a table, gulp it down. Moments later he'd start stumbling, sometimes falling down. As soon as he'd had the least bit of alcohol, he was finished.

A short while later a friend called me and said, "Have you seen Bud Powell lately? He's begging on the street." I couldn't believe it. But sure enough, I found him on the boulevard St. Germain, asking passers-by for spare change. At this point I became so upset that I decided to act, to do something. People treated him like a bum, Buttercup treated him like a dog. They'd throw him out of the club, and Buttercup would bring him back to the hotel and lock him in his room until the next day. He only left his room in the evenings to play in the club. At this point I began to invite him into our home. I had to get permission from Buttercup to do this.

As soon as he was in our place, however, I noticed a change. He ate with a big appetite, started to smile, appeared happy. We had a piano at home, and he was happy to hear me play his compositions. He would play too. It was also around this time that I noticed that Buttercup would give him little pink pills. When I asked her about them, she told me, "It's his medication. He has to take it every day." Shortly after that I took one of these little pills and had it analyzed. It turned out to be a medication called Largactyl, a very powerful tranquilizer given to extreme cases in psychiatric hospitals. It turns whoever takes it into a zombie, makes it impossible for them to make any decisions. It puts you into a type of hypnotic state where you are completely dependent upon others.

So here was this genius living on the streets, being put into the hospital or thrown in jail, and people didn't seem to give a damn. Each time Bud disappeared—it happened several times a week—Buttercup would call me saying, "See what you can do." Once Bud was taken to the Laennec hospital. They had gotten his medical dossier from the American Embassy and they knew everything about his life in hospitals and jails. So they decided to put him in a psychiatric cell. I went to the hospital and explained to the doctors who this man was, and I guess I was pretty good, because they let Bud go out with me. At this very moment, I decided, with Bud's agreement, to take him to my home.

TS: What was your life with Bud like?
FP: Bud was actually a very calm person. In fact life became easier and more relaxed with him here. I could do my daily work in my home studio as a designer without having to worry about Bud, or run around looking for him any more. I would make him his breakfast, usually eggs, then we'd listen to music, laugh together. He'd ask me, "What are you going to work on today?" Then he'd sit down next to me and watch all day long. We'd listen to Art Tatum records. From time to time he'd go to the piano to check out a chord or two, then come back to watch me at the drawing board. Then in the evening my wife Nicole would return from work, and we'd

have dinner together. He enjoyed peaceful surroundings. He was looking for peace. He didn't talk much but smiled. He was in his dreams.

TS: Did he stop taking the medication?

FP: Yes, I had him decrease the dosage gradually and finally stop, under the supervision of a doctor friend. I noticed that after he'd stopped, he could better tolerate and enjoy a little glass of wine with dinner. I found out that the association of Largactyl and alcohol was responsible for his behavior, as well as abusive medical prescriptions in hospitals.

TS: Did he play the piano at home?

FP: Not a lot. The music was inside of him. I would see his fingers or feet move. I didn't know much about his musical background, so I began to ask him questions about it. He told me he'd studied a lot of classical piano. In reality he had been a young virtuoso and had wanted to become a classical pianist. He played a solo classical concert at Carnegie Hall at fifteen, then a second there with another jazz pianist, Elmo Hope. Another pianist, Walter Davis, Jr., remembers Bud playing classical pieces in his house at Willow Grove, Pennsylvania.

TS: Why did Bud leave your home?

FP: I had to send him to the sanatorium, because after routine medical examination, we found out that he had contracted tuberculosis a long time ago and his health was getting worse and worse. The seven months he spent there cost a fortune and there was no way he could pay. He had no medical insurance, no royalties, no fees—Buttercup was getting them when he was working. So I agreed to pay for it and the doctors and staff were wonderful. They accepted monthly payments until the bill was covered. Bud was completely cured and in good health. It was a resurrection. In fact, he had transformed completely. All the American jazzmen—Jackie McLean, Duke Ellington, Max Roach, Sonny Rollins, Thelonious Monk—who came to Paris would say, "We saw Bud Powell over there and you wouldn't believe your eyes! He is not the same person you used to know!"

It was around this time that Oscar Goodstein in New York

invited Bud to come and play Birdland. Goodstein's argument to Bud was that since he had enormous bills to pay off, why not come to New York and play?" People want to hear you. and you'll have recording sessions and record deals!" he said. Goodstein also invited me to come along, feeling that Bud would be more protected and feel more confident with me there. It seemed like a good idea. Bud was still known as a great pianist, and since Charlie Parker was dead and Monk was in a kind of routine, it seemed like the jazz world in America would greet Bud's return like children would greet the return of Santa Claus.

TS: This was in 1964?

FP: Yes, and Bud was in good health. He'd found a new *joie de vivre*. For my part, I was a little naive. I didn't know the harder side of life in New York City since I'd never been there. When I talked to Bud about going back to New York he became excited too. I told him, "Bird isn't there. Billie Holiday isn't there, Lester isn't there. You have to go back. You'll give them back something they've been missing." Bud was also excited that I'd be going back with him, happy to show me around his world and home town. I wanted him to make a triumphant return to the American jazz scene, a different and much stronger man, and a better artist than when he left for Europe, demonstrating the power of friendship to a society torn by racism. So we left for America.

The first thing Oscar Goodstein told us when we got there was that Bud owed money to the musician's union, and to him, and to his lawyers, and that the airline tickets, hotel, and so on, were up to us to pay. Three and a half months later when I finally returned to Paris, I was indebted by $2000 more than before we came.

TS: When you left New York did you have the impression that it would be the last time you would see Bud?

FP: The end was dramatic. Bud rediscovered all the pressure inherent in New York life—the indifference of people, their opportunism, their unwillingness to get involved. Bud had many flashbacks of what he'd lived through there before— the beating by policemen on a case of mistaken identity, the incarcerations at Bellevue and Creedmore, the fact that so many drug dealers were around. One day without telling me, Bud took off to see his father, whom he hadn't seen in a long time. His father telephoned me and screamed, "I don't want him here!! Get him out! I had too much trouble in the past!" That was the definitive kayo that ended it for Bud.

From then on he started getting depressed all the time, he started drinking again. I said, "Dammit Bud, for six months you haven't been drinking. Is it starting all over again?" He jumped at every occasion to drink. I had to get back to Paris and start working again, because I was broke by this time and had to start paying off these enormous debts. I had a small child and needed to see what he looked like. Bud was his godfather. So we decided to go back to Paris.

After a recording session arranged by Oscar Goodstein, we got the money to buy our tickets. At that time, we were staying with the Baroness Nica de Koenigswarter. I called Bud's daughter, Celia, and her mother Frances, and told them to come and say goodbye. Our flight was early the next day. They arrived at Nica's late in the evening, with Frances's sister.

After a while, Frances's sister—who had never come to the club and did not even give a call during our three month stay—started doing a mumber on Bud. "Why don't you stay with us, Bud? We are your family! Remember the time I cooked red beans and rice for you?" and so on. Bud began to hesitate and finally asked me if he could stay with them that last night. I said, "Okay, but remember, we leave tomorrow early in the morning. We already postponed five times and I've got to go back."

So we decided to meet at the airport. [Pianist] Barry Harris took me to the airport and we both waited for Bud. He didn't show up, which I had been afraid of. I knew he would be finished if he stayed in New York, but I had to go. So I left Bud's suitcase and ticket with Barry. A week later, Bud was already in a hospital! He had met Margareta, a Swedish girl who worked for Atlantic Records and whom he wanted to marry. She kept me informed about the situation, in spite of her difficulties in getting to see Bud. Gil Evans, the great arranger and composer, also kept me up on the news about Bud.

After some time, my financial situation had improved and I was ready to go to New York and take Bud back with me when I read an article saying that Bud was in King's County Hospital, in bad shape. I asked Margareta for more information and she confirmed he was sick and not able to travel. So I postponed my trip and worked hard to calm my anxiety. A few days later, after a busy day, I finally went to bed with a bad feeling—I did not know why.

No sooner had I fallen asleep than I woke up in a weird state. I got up, started to pace around my apartment, and smoked all the cigarettes I had, without being able to control myself. So I decided to go back to bed, but my sleep was troubled. Shortly after, a small, familiar sound woke me. It came from the mailbox in the door. I am a graphic designer and I am always getting things delivered through this mail slot. I got up and looked in. In the shade, I could see the light blue envelope of a telegram.

I opened and read, "Bud is no longer with us. He died at 21:40 this evening." Figuring in the time difference between Paris and New York, this was exactly the time when I was startled out of my sleep by that terrible premonition.

It was as if something had snapped in the universe.
[Note: Bud Powell died July 31st, 1966 in New York.]

[Francis Paudras' account of his life with Bud Powell is contained in his extraordinary biography, *La Danse des Infidels* (Paris, L'Instant, 1986).]

Translated by Tom Schnabel.

1988

PENGUIN CAFE ORCHESTRA

T HE PENGUIN CAFE ORCHESTRA IS A DELIGHTFULLY ECLECTIC group first championed by Brian Eno. If you haven't heard them yet, imagine a blend of chamber, cajun, balalaika, Hawaiian and rock, played on Bosendorfer pianos, harmoniums, ukeleles, milkbottles, cowbells, solobans (!) and metal plates. My conversation one bright April day with founder Simon Jeffes, a music school dropout, preceded a sold out PCO concert that night.

TS: Simon, you just said off-mike that if you see corned beef hash on the menu, it must be the States.

SJ: That's one of the perks of coming to America, I think. Civilization.

TS: I understand the group got its name from a bad experience in France.

SJ: Yes, indirectly. I first came across the idea of a Penguin Cafe after I'd had food poisoning. And as I lay in bed feeling very sick, nauseous, I had this vision in my mind that wouldn't go away. It was quite clearly some time in the future, a vision of a possible future for us. There was this concrete building

"A poem spontaneously leapt out:
I am the proprietor of the Penguin Cafe.
I will tell you things at random . . ."

which had this electronic eye watching everything. In all the rooms people were taken up with self-interest. They weren't a threat to the prevailing order.

One of the examples was a musician with a synthesizer, a huge machine with headphones and keyboards, and he was in ecstasy making all this music. But there was no sound at all. This place was totally silent. It was chillingly bleak, the atmosphere. Terrible. There was no life. Everybody was dealt with. I was sitting on a beach a couple of days after that. A poem spontaneously leapt out: "I am the proprietor of the Penguin Cafe. I will tell you things at random . . ." And this voice just blabbed away for five pages, which is quite unusual for me because I don't write poetry. Something quite strong came out.

The gist of what he said was that the spontaneous, random, unpredictable element in our lives is very important, and that if you start to squash it because you're afraid—for instance, you might suppress it because of insecurity about a parent, random acts of terrorism, threats—you want to start to tighten up on society. And if you allow that to happen, you start to lose something that's precious. So he was saying that that can't happen here. This is the Penguin Cafe. So he invited you to come to the Penguin Cafe, and that was the origin.

TS: You guys have been together for quite some time.

SJ: In 1972 I went to Japan. It was there that the idea of the orchestra really started to develop, because I started to write about the cafe. Naturally there would be music in the cafe. When I came back to England in '73, I got together with musicians and we started to play in the spirit of the Penguin Cafe.

TS: If you met a buyer in a record store, how would you characterize your music?

SJ: Categorizing Penguin music is really difficult. It's just about everything. If I was to describe it I would say it's contemporary instrumental music which has the good things of classical music and folk music and rock in it, in a fairly new way. Its newness doesn't mean that it's dissonant or aggressive. It's actually consonant and harmonious.

TS: You guys were a big success in Japan.

SJ: I conceived of the orchestra in Japan. Then exactly ten years after my first visit we went back again, this time with the Penguin Cafe Orchestra. The first time I'd been writing about it as a kind of fiction, an ideal. The second time I went there with the orchestra. We had an album on the charts there. It was quite an extraordinary thing. I had really learned something from their culture which kept me going for ten years. So when our album came out there, it was by coincidence the Year of the Penguin in Japan. They have a kind of trendy animal of the year that they get obsessed about, either a panda or a parakeet. That's not the only reason our album did well, but it was symptomatic.

TS: "The Ecstasy of Dancing Fleas" is, I believe, from your second record.

SJ: Do you know why it's called "The Ecstasy of Dancing Fleas?"

TS: No.

SJ: "Ukelele" in Hawaiian means "dancing fleas." The word "ecstasy" is from the Greek, meaning "stand outside of yourself." So the title really means "stand outside of yourself with a ukelele." In other words, to go into a trance-like state with a ukelele in your hand.

TS: Do you write all the music down? There's really no improvisation or solos?

SJ: There's a kind of balance of structure and improvisation. The thing I've always felt about the music is that it's not a straitjacket, it's not a template. It's a set of music principles. Some specific lines have to be played, but they can be played in the manner that the individual wants.

TS: Have there been other musicians or composers you've particularly admired? There are so many influences in your orchestra, from Cajun to balalaika, Hawaiian, and chamber music of course.

SJ: Almost too many. I suppose mine would include Beethoven and Cajun music and Satie and Ravel, Stravinsky, Arvo Pärt. And I've got a record of Madagascar zither music which is extraordinary. Some *kora* music. Very specific tracks on very specific records. It's not like ethnic music is a massive, total turn-on. But you find treasures in it, just like pop music.

1988

STOLEN MOMENTS

*"She said, 'This is Astor Piazzolla. Don't ever leave it.'
Since that day I started believing in Astor Piazzolla."*

ASTOR PIAZZOLLA

ASTOR PIAZZOLLA HAS DEVOTED HIS LIFE TO THE MUSICAL SOUL *of Argentina, the tango. As Buenos Aires' most important bandoneonista, he has extended the boundaries of the tango, often against fierce opposition. What Carlos Gardel made internationally popular in the 1930's, Piazzolla has made a contemporary artform.*

The bandoneon *is accordion-like, but with no piano keyboard, only buttons on both sides. Small at first glance, it opens up to be almost five feet wide: the instrument par excellence of tango. As Piazzolla, dressed entirely in black, plays with an intense countenance, the instrument develops a serpentine quality, the music deep, moody and mysterious.*

TS: You were born in Argentina, but you grew up in Little Italy, correct?

AP: Yes. It's very surrealistic, my life. I was born in Mar de Plata, four hundred kilometers from Buenos Aires. In 1923 my father went to see New York. He came back after two weeks and took my mother and me there. We lived fourteen years in New York.

TS: Did growing up in New York City affect your music?

AP: I'm sure about that. Not in the way I compose, not in the way I play. I like contemporary jazz very much. I was playing George Gershwin on my instrument, the bandoneon. So I have the feeling of jazz inside of me. But I can't write jazz. To write jazz you must be a jazz musician, or live in the United States. I feel the tango because my father had around fifty or sixty 78 rpm records, and they were all tangos. Very good orchestras. My father used to listen to them every night and he would cry. I looked at him and I couldn't imagine why he cried. Then he said, "This is the music that I feel, that I love most. This is the music from Argentina. This is the tango."

And little by little, fourteen years listening to that music every evening when my father came back from work and put this music on, I started to feel it myself also. So that's why I go back to Argentina and I get struck by this music called the tango. But the ones who wanted to strike me were the traditional tango players, who didn't like my way of playing.

TS: What about the classical music coming from the apartment next door?

AP: Yes, I used to sit in my back yard in New York and listen to a pianist who was a Hungarian concert player. His name was Bela Wilda. He studied with Sergei Rachmaninoff, and he used to play three or four hours of Bach every morning. I used to get up and open the window and listen to this man play piano. And I told my mother I wanted to study music with this man, not with the other man who wanted to teach me to play tangos. So I went to study with Bela Wilda, and he adapted all piano music to my instrument, the bandoneon. The piano has eighty eight notes, and the bandoneon has seventy eight. It's nearly like a piano. So I started playing Bach, Schumann, Mozart. My beginning was all classical music.

TS: Do you play the melodies with your right hand and the chords and bass notes with your left hand?

AP: No. You can do everything with both hands. I mean, sometimes one hand alone is okay, but this is such a complicated instrument. It has four techniques. The left hand has two techniques—opening sounds one way, and when you close it it's different. On the right hand it's exactly the same thing—you open it's one sound, you close it it's another. It's not like the piano, where you only have one. But I learned it. It was important that I study the bandoneon because it opened my brains a little more.

TS: So in New York City you said, "Dad, I want a bandoneon?" And he had to send to Buenos Aires?

AP: No, he found it in a pawn shop in New York. It was my birthday. He paid eighteen dollars for a very old bandoneon. It was nearly a concertina in those times. And I started studying the next day.

TS: Where are bandoneons made? Are they Italian originally, or are they Argentine?

AP: The story of the bandoneon is very strange. It was invented in 1854 in Karlfelt, Germany, to play religious music in a very small church, because they didn't have any money to buy an organ. So the bandoneon has a very sad, melancholic sound. The left hand especially sounds like an organ. By 1890 it was in the whorehouses of Buenos Aires, playing tango. Then from the bordellos, it went into the concert halls. So it went all around, the bandoneon. Then I went back and played it in the church in Karlfelt. (laughs)

TS: You met Carlos Gardel in New York in 1934, didn't you?

AP: Yes. It was very special. We were ten Argentines living in New York then, and when Carlos got there it was like God coming to New York. He was the best tango singer. And my father, who used to make sculptures on wood, made a sculpture of an Argentine gaucho playing the guitar, and he dedicated it to Carlos Gardel. I went to his hotel and I gave him this sculpture from my father, and all of a sudden when he found out I was playing the bandoneon he nearly fainted, because he couldn't find a bandoneon player any place, especially not in New York. I wasn't the best bandoneon player, I was the only bandoneon player! (laughs).

So I was playing all classical music, and he said, "Can you play a tango?" I said, "If I could play Johann Sebastian Bach I can play a tango. It's much easier." "Okay. We have to do a recording." We did a recording of one of his last films. All the Gardel films were very famous in Latin America. It was the first time I played a tango in my life. And this year the opera company of Philadelphia commissioned me to write an opera on the life of Carlos Gardel. It's about 54 years from his death. There's a possibility that Placido Domingo will play Carlos Gardel.

TS: Nadia Boulanger [composition teacher based in Paris] had a decisive influence on your life, didn't she?

AP: She was my second mother. She didn't only teach me music, she taught me life. She taught me to believe in myself. She told me to throw the classical music that I wrote into the garbage. "Throw it away. This is no good. I can't find Piazzolla in this classical concert music." She wanted to know what I really did in life for a living. I was very much ashamed to tell her that I played tango, and above all I wouldn't dare to say to Nadia, "I play the bandoneon." I thought she would throw me out the window. I was there studying like Aaron Copland, like Leonard Bernstein, and Igor Markevitch. How can I say to this old and wonderful lady that I was playing tango in a cafe in Buenos Aires? All of a sudden I had this moment of courage and I said, "Look, Miss Boulanger"—she was 75 years old then—"Look," I said, with my head bending down, "I play tango." "Oh," she says, "that's beautiful."

I was amazed at her answer, but she loved tango. She started naming all the tangos she knew—Stravinsky's, and Darius Milhaud's—so many important composers in the world wrote tangos. She said, "You don't play piano?" "No," I said, "I just use piano for composing." "What do you play?" I was again ashamed, and I said, "I play the bandoneon." She said, "Oh, I love the bandoneon. Did you hear Kurt Weill when he played the bandoneon?" "Yes," I said. "Boris Blacher also used the bandoneon, and Hindemith wrote for the bandoneon." And she asked me to play a few bars of a tango. She wanted to know about my tangos. I played a little bit of my tangos, and she took my two hands together and she said, "This is Astor Piazzolla. Don't ever leave it."

Since that day I started believing in Astor Piazzolla and I threw away all the music I had written. I thought I was a genius because I wrote symphonies, but I wasn't a genius because I wasn't Astor Piazzolla.

1988

STOLEN MOMENTS

*"When I got out of graduate school
I got a job with the Yellow Cab Company,
since my financial future was dubious . . ."*

STEVE REICH

I STILL GET PHONE CALLS WHEN I PLAY STEVE REICH'S MUSIC, *helpfully informing me that the record is skipping. I want to tell them to listen again, there's a subtle magic unfolding. Listening to Reich is like looking at an insect: When you're standing up it just looks like a bug, but if you kneel down and look closely, all of a sudden you'll see its iridescence, its colorful striations, the lovely sheen of its carapace.*

Unlike Philip Glass, with whom he is sometimes compared, Steve Reich's music is completely acoustic and relies far more on texture than dynamics. Like Glass, however, Reich is thoroughly familiar with the full range of modern music from all cultures, from Junior Walker to Burundi chants.

TS: Steve, what do you demand from your musicians? They have to be special to understand the nuances and the dynamics of your music, to be able to listen. I guess you're asking the same thing of your listeners, too.

SR: The players are pretty much all people who've gone through the better conservatories in this country. Then something has happened to them after that. (laughs) They've decided not to become orchestral players, certainly, and they've gotten interested in some other form of music. Indian music, African music, jazz, rock. That is the kind of musician who seems to end up in the ensemble.

TS: Are you trying to get a certain response? Are you trying to get people high?

SR: Well, in the sense in which all good music gets people high, yes. I think when people listen to my music they bring the ears they bring to any other kind of music. If the music needs explanations and a special psychological preparation for listening, then there must be something wrong with the music. A naive response is the best. People may find that they begin to hear details of sound that they don't normally pay attention to.

TS: Are you a native New Yorker?

SR: Believe it or not, I am.

TS: Where did you study?

SR: Well, I've been through a lot of schooling. I went to Cornell and studied music and philosophy. Then I went down to New York and studied privately with Hall Overton, who was both a classical musician and a jazz musician, a good friend of Thelonious Monk, and one of the best teachers I ever had. I went to Julliard for three years. Then I went out to the West Coast, Mills College, where Luciano Berio from Italy had just arrived, and Darius Milhaud, who was old and not in such great health, was teaching. I was there from 1961 to '63. I stayed in the Bay Area until 1965, then went back to New York.

TS: Critics have talked about the freshness of your music, that it's something new, an antidote to the stultifying academic atmosphere of contemporary classical music. Your music also appeals to a popular audience that goes out and buys Brian Eno, Talking Heads, and Peter Gabriel records. Did you know that it would just be a matter of time before people would appreciate your music when you were first composing?

SR: To tell you the truth, I had no idea. When I got out of graduate school I got a job with the Yellow Cab Company, since my financial future was dubious. (laughs) My first ensemble was basically friends who would play my music, and they were the only ones who would. So the ensemble was not some kind of a master plan to survive with. But I think it has turned out that I've survived—economically, at least—by being connected with the performance of my music. If I had just written and not performed I would have had to do something else to survive. Having an ensemble has been the crucial factor.

But believe it or not, back in the late '50's and early '60's people were naive and idealistic enough to not even know how they would survive. I guess the world was a little bit different then, certainly economically more optimistic in outlook, and one could sort of forget where you were going to make a living and let the chips fall where they may. It turned out that starting in '71 I began to survive by playing my own music.

TS: Do you resent the use of the term "minimalist" that critics have applied to your work?

SR: Basically, it's a handle. You can't pick up a hot teacup, your fingers burn unless you have a handle. People say "impressionism" in music, I know they're talking about Debussy, maybe Ravel. When people talk about minimalism I know they're talking about me and Phil Glass and Terry Riley, and maybe La Monte Young. And in that sense it's useful, because it's shorthand to say a bunch of different names.

TS: Taken from the visual arts.

SR: Yeah. People like Frank Stella, Sol LeWitt, Don Judd. I think it describes earlier pieces of mine, let's say *Four Organs* or *Violin Phase*, where there's very little change and things go on for twenty minutes or half hour with not much of a change. Starting with *Music for Mallets, Instruments, Voices and Organ*, or certainly *Music for Eighteen Musicians* in '76, I think it gets to be less descriptive, since there are considerably more traditional things we look for in Western music—changes of instruments, changes of harmony and so on. But the word has stuck. It's obviously going to be around

and I don't mind living with it.
TS: Listening to the music, you hear something new. That's the appeal of your music. But in fact you are using certain traditions that are thousands of years old.
SR: That's true too.
TS: I want you to talk a little bit about the *gamelan,* which was an influence on Debussy ninety years ago, as well as drumming from Ghana. Percussion plays a more important role in your music than anything else, doesn't it?
SR: Yes, I'd say it does. I was a drummer when I was fourteen. I studied with Roland Koloff who is now the tympanist with the New York Philharmonic. I think the impetus to stop piano and study drums was unquestionably jazz, and the drummer who I remember thinking was the greatest in the world was Kenny Clarke, who many of your younger listeners may not know. He was a jazz bebop drummer, a very, very great one. What struck me about Kenny Clarke was not his virtuosity, which he didn't have and which I don't either, but his sense of time. He would make the entire band float as if it was effortlessly pulsating in the air.

The desire for that kind of musical time has remained with me ever since. I started studying drums then, and I would say that what instrumental talents I have are certainly percussive, and that my basic impetus towards music is percussive. My music since 1965 clearly shows that. When you feel that way and you are a music student in the West and you've gone to music school with music teachers like Luciano Berio, who is a twelve tone composer, and you wonder, "how can drumming in a popular sense have anything to do with classical music?", the logical place to turn—if you are fortunate enough to turn there—is Africa, because in Africa the drums, the rattles, the xylophones play the role in their music that strings do in the Western orchestra. There is singing, there are occasionally string instruments. But the dominant voice is the drum.

The other culture that has percussion front and center is Indonesia. And of the two major musical cultures over there I was more drawn to Bali rather than to Java. Perhaps Java is more slow-moving, more elegant harmonically, and Bali is certainly more intricate, more active rhythmically. I'd heard African drumming and Balinese gamelan since my teens but I'd had no idea what was going on. How did any human being make that sound? In 1962 I was studying with Berio. At night I was at the Jazz Workshop in San Francisco listening to John Coltrane, who at that period of time was playing an awful lot of music on very few harmonies. That made an enormous impression on me. In pop music you had Junior Walker's "Shotgun," which was one bass line repeating throughout the whole tune.

This kind of thing was in the air. Non-Western music, jazz and rock music were at that time moving toward very few harmonies. Then everybody in Berio's class went down to Ojai, near here, to a composer's conference. One of the composers was Gunther Schuller. He was writing his history of early jazz in America. He was talking about the book and he wanted to know what American blacks had done before they came here, and lo and behold he discovered a book called *Studies in African Music* by an Englishman named A.M. Jones, published by the Oxford University Press. So I ran back to the Berkeley library, got that two-volume set out—which is one volume of scores and one volume of commentary—and that really opened my mind, because I saw how this music is made.

It is repeating patterns, basically divisions of what we would call twelve-eight, with down beats staggered, so they don't come on one particular beat. If you ask the various drummers in the ensemble, "Where's the down beat?" you'll get a different story from each. There's no one down beat as we have in the West. There's another book called *Music in Bali*, by the Canadian composer and musicologist Colin McPhee, which showed me that many of the techniques I was using were also used in Bali. I don't think it was a case of going to Africa and learning how to do something and running back and doing the piece called "Drumming." I was a drummer, I was looking for encouragement.

People ask me, "What did you get from Africa?" and the

answer is a pat on the back, big confirmations. Yes, you can make acoustical music. Yes, you can use percussion instruments and they will be as complex and rich in sound as any electronic ensemble that you can imagine, and there is a tradition over there that dates back thousands of years that uses percussion to create their classical music. The music that I'm talking about here is the music used for religious occasions, for the installation of a chief. Certainly they have good-times-get-drunk music, and that uses drums too. That was interesting—whether it's classic or popular it swings. And all African music swings.

1986

ROBBIE ROBERTSON

THE BREAKUP OF THE BAND AFTER A CONCERT EXTRAVAGANZA *at San Francisco's Winterland in 1976, immortalized in Martin Scorcese's film* The Last Waltz, *symbolized the end of an era. The group had risen to prominence backing Bob Dylan, then made several landmark albums of their own. The death a few years ago of Richard Manuel, the group's pianist, dashed any hopes of comeback LP's or concerts; then a long-awaited solo album by Robbie Robertson, The Band's main composer and guitarist, arrived. This was the occasion for our conversation, but he spoke of other things, including the changing American landscape and his own Indian roots.*

TS: How do you like being back in the limelight?
RR: I don't think about limelight very much. What I do think about is trying to do some good work. I'm giving it everything I've got, and that's what comes to the front for me. Limelight, I don't know. Once you do it I don't think it particularly goes away. It always stays somewhere in the back of your mind, whether you're coming out or going in.

STOLEN MOMENTS

"You take a kid from driving a truck, and suddenly his music and his image is controlling the world . . . I don't think that's a real healthy existence."

I've enjoyed the idea of playing the disappearing man for a while and working from an underground point of view, working with films and everything. It doesn't seem like, "My goodness! Here I am again!"

TS: You said once that you didn't want to do another album until you had some songs, something to say. You characterized people who do one album each year as churning out pulp. It's something I sort of agree with. On the other hand, you arrived in Dublin to work with U2 with just little scraps of paper in your pocket for the songs on your new album. What was happening, anyway?

RR: I wasn't overly prepared. But I was on kind of a roll. I was maybe halfway through this album. I had stopped to do the music for *The Color of Money* for Martin Scorcese. And you always think it isn't going to take as much time as it does. I didn't have that extra period that I thought I would to sit down and write and prepare. I thought out of due respect I should go over there with something in my hand. But it was just a musical experiment we were talking about. It wasn't like, "Okay, we're definitely going to do some songs for your album." We had just talked about mixing these worlds of music together, which is something I've always liked to do since years ago when I did it with Bob Dylan and Van Morrison. And in *The Last Waltz* I did it with everybody you can imagine. I think it's how rock and roll came about, too, mixing a little blues, a little boogie, a little country, and "bingo . . ."

So when I went there I was concerned, because they were thinking of me as this guy who wrote songs and that I would be prepared. But it didn't seem to bother anybody terribly. I did have these scraps of paper, and a couple of little ideas on cassette that just had enough clues to get everybody in the mood, at least. And they were so enthusiastic and encouraging that it didn't seem to be a problem. I think they pride themselves a little bit on their own spontaneous capabilities. So we put them to the test.

TS: Robbie, you characterize your music as an attempt to explore American mythology. You talk about "shadowland"

and things like that. Could you tell us a little more about that?

RR: For me it was something that I was always intrigued with, this country being so young that we can't have those resources to call upon like they do in Rome and in Greece. I think we're discovering our mythology as we go along, and drawing upon the American Indian reality and myth, up to present-day things. For me it was a great tool. I found a large canvas there. There was something very rich in the soil to choose from. Rather than being confined, I felt that this was a very broad horizon. It made me feel good, too, to be part of something that I felt was being discovered, or discovering it through music.

TS: You were born in Canada. Where, exactly?

RR: Toronto.

TS: And you have native American ancestry on your mother's side.

RR: My mother was born on the Sioux Nation Indian reservation in the tobacco belt in Canada—which is very near where Daniel Lanois comes from, actually.

TS: Do you think that affected you? You spent your summers on the reservation with your mom, observing a very different way of life.

RR: Yeah. It was a very musical environment too. Everybody seemed to play something, which was my first tap into that—seeing somebody sitting right next to you with an instrument, as opposed to on a stage somewhere or just listening to it on the radio. I thought, "Boy, I've got to be a part of this some day." It's where I got my first guitar lessons.

TS: Do you think your native American descent on your mother's side affected this whole idea of a mythology of American roots?

RR: You never know. I've never chosen to over-think it, but I'm sure that it did. These people seemed to have a very beautiful balance with nature, a connection with the earth. You felt this was really special, something about these people and the way they are family-oriented.

TS: It's interesting, going back to The Band, that there you were in the middle of the Vietnam War and everything else, playing songs that didn't take a stand against it. Yet your records and songs were tremendously successful. It's interesting also that there's even the word—what do they call it, "heartland rock"?—that the critics are bandying about now, with Springsteen and everything else. It's something you've been doing for a long time.

RR: Yeah, I was writing patriotic songs at that time. It wasn't very in vogue then. Now I feel the opposite. I don't know, I just can't seem to get into the mainstream.

TS: In *The Last Waltz,* you used a string of adjectives—the last one was "psychotic"—to describe the whole lifestyle on the road with The Band. Was that the way it was?

RR: Well, there was a period starting somewhere in the late sixties—maybe in the middle sixties, but I think it came to some kind of a peak in the late sixties and early seventies—where this road lifestyle was driving very close to the edge for a lot of people. It's pretty evident now what a toll it's taken. I get a feeling from some young musicians coming up now that it's quite different. It makes me feel very good to hear that from them. The whole idea of trying to see how rough you can live, how fast and how far you can take it, is not necessarily the point anymore. Maybe it's got more to do with trying to do your best work and survive. I think it's great that we've learned something, hopefully, from all of this.

There are a couple of songs on this album—one is "American Roulette"—which was thematically connected with this. I often thought, in the writing of this song, that these people—I deal with the legends of Marilyn Monroe and Elvis Presley and James Dean in this song—didn't die for nothing. I think that there's something passed on to everybody else, for younger artists coming up to say, "Uh-huh. See what happens when you do this? You don't understand that, you drive into the wall." You take a kid from driving a truck and you put him in this situation where his music and his image is all of a sudden controlling the world to a certain extent. Then he realizes he can't go out of the house for the next twenty five years. I don't think that's a real healthy existence.

TS: So obviously life on the road was one of the reasons why you needed to take time off.

RR: Yes. Sometimes you even feel maybe a little superstitious about it. You think, "How many rides on this merry go round do you get before you fall off?" It had a lot to do with me thinking I'd like to bring that chapter to a conclusion.

TS: Your fans, and the fans of The Band, don't let you forget anything, do they?

RR: No they don't, Tom.

TS: Does that come back to haunt you sometimes?

RR: No, not really. If anything, it makes me feel good that there are people that care that much. I feel proud of a lot of that work that I did with The Band. But I also like the idea of fresh ears out there, and conquering new horizons. It's all exciting.

TS: Your song "Show Down at Big Sky" certainly is more politically-oriented than the songs you used to write for The Band.

RR: Well, differently politically-oriented, anyway. With this nuclear horror, we have these leaders meeting, talking about destroying eight billion dollars in weapons. Boy, we sure could have fed a few people with that money. I had been contemplating this idea about writing this song, and I went back and forth on it, thinking, "I should do it. Ahhh, who needs this? Who wants to hear about this any more?" Then I got really angry at myself for even questioning the idea. Everybody should do whatever they possibly can to make that small contribution. It all adds up.

So I ended up going through with it, but trying to find a little more spiritual angle, not trying to be preachy or hit it over the head. The idea of a counterpoint in the song helped me, bringing it down to the simplicity of the early American Indian way of life, and using spiritual, biblical terms. Counterpointing that with soldiers of fortune. They get hired and sent into these countries just to stir up some dust. It's a horrible game being played. We know that there are zillions of dollars being made in building weapons, and it's a hard fight to stop something like that. But it's nice to see these guys getting together and at least talking about it. How are they going to destroy all these weapons, I wonder. Where are they going to put them? Dig a big hole somewhere?

TS: Is music a spiritual force for you, Robbie?

RR: Yeah, it is. I'm not plugging any kind of religious format, but I'm certainly a fan of great storytelling, and in the Bible there's tremendous storytelling. In American mythology as we discover it there's great storytelling. So sometimes these two and the writing must meet. I've always liked the resonance of those lyrics, sometimes in other people, too. You've heard the things that Van Morrison has written, and you say, "I don't know what this man is talking about, but whatever it is, it's fantastic." It's the resonance, and I get that sometimes — like this song, "Show Down at Big Sky." I don't know where "the valley of tears" is or what "the book of David" is. But I seem to understand something about it when I hear it. "It will be written by the children of Eden." Calling upon those kind of forces through those lyrics, I feel more thunder.

TS: You're talking more like an American Indian conception of God being already there, in the ground. Do you believe in God?

RR: I believe in that God. I just spent some time in New Mexico, in this place, Acoma. It's an Indian reservation that's been there for a thousand years. I shot two videos there. It's built on top of a mesa, a magnificent place. When you stand up there, you say, "Oh yeah. No question about this." (laughs) You can feel it, and it makes the outside world, the cities and everything, feel petty in comparison with this connection with the earth and the sky. These wonderful people feel, "Well, you take care of mother nature and mother nature will take care of you." There seems to be a great lesson to be learned from these people that we've lost along the way.

TS: You started writing the song "Fallen Angel," and as you wrote, it became more and more a song about a departed friend.

RR: I didn't know what I was writing about for quite a while. Maybe I just didn't want to face the fact. We have this little built-in wall against those things sometimes. When I did come to terms with what the song's about, it felt good to me to face up to it. It was a cleansing feeling to write this song in honor of a friend of mine who died. [Richard Manuel, former Band member, had taken his life.]

TS: Do you have any interests outside of music?

RR: I'd like to take some time to go around the country and go to Indian ceremonials, because you can't tape them and you can't put them on film or videotape. A lot of them, unless you're Indian yourself, you can't see. It's very, very sacred. This is my most haunting private passion at the moment.

1988

RYUICHI SAKAMOTO

IF JAPAN IS ASCENDANT IN GLOBAL ECONOMICS, ITS MUSIC SCENE *is equally alive, diverse, and full of energy. Perhaps no contemporary Japanese musician has gone further toward establishing an international identity than Ryuichi Sakamoto. A pop idol in Japan who can't go out in the Tokyo streets without being mobbed, Sakamoto is best known elsewhere as an actor and composer. In Los Angeles to pick up a Golden Globe Award for his soundtrack for* The Last Emperor, *composed with David Byrne (it would also win the Oscar), he visited with me in the studio. The conversation was at times oblique, Zen-like.*

- *TS:* Congratulations for winning the Golden Globe Award for the soundtrack to *The Last Emperor*.
- *RS:* Thank you very much.
- *TS:* You were born in Tokyo?
- *RS:* In 1952.
- *TS:* And what got you interested in music?
- *RS:* I don't know. My uncle is a very maniac music fan. But he didn't get me interested. My first memory of music is Men-

STOLEN MOMENTS

"I would like to use Jimi Hendrix for guitar . . .
Coltrane for solo parts.
And strings from The Berlin Philharmonic."

delssohn's *Violin Concert Number One*. I remember I started to play piano when I was three or four, and continued.

TS: Was there music on the radio at home?

RS: Oh, yes.

TS: I understand you weren't ever interested in becoming a professional musician.

RS: Yes.

TS: You've done a pretty good job of it.

RS: It's kind of an accident. (Laughs)

TS: Then I was wondering what inspired you to become one.

RS: Old classics, old pop, old rock, old jazz, movies, art. The Beatles, Rolling Stones, Johann Sebastian Bach, Debussy, Beethoven, Coltrane, Warhol, Godard.

TS: So those are the people who made you become a musician?

RS: Not a professional musician, but they made me interested in music.

TS: Did you study classical piano? The conservatory, the whole thing?

RS: Yeah. From Bach to Debussy, Ravel.

TS: Did Debussy influence you musically?

RS: Very much, yes. My first contact with Debussy was his string quartet when I was fourteen, I think. At the same time I heard Ravel's "String Quartet." I liked both, but Debussy's better.

TS: It's got that great middle movement.

RS: Yes. Before that I loved Beethoven. Of course I was shocked by Debussy, the harmony and melody, the delicacy. I didn't know about French classical music before that.

TS: You first achieved fame with the Yellow Magic Orchestra, the first Japanese pop group to become popular in America. When and how did Yellow Magic Orchestra come together?

RS: We had tried to make Japanese techno-pop, which was invented by Kraftwerk, a German group.

TS: What fascinates you the most about technology?

RS: To me, technology is just a tool for making music. For example, I can make music with acoustic piano. That's my music. That means I don't need new technology for making

my music. But it's fun to play with the technology.
TS: What is the most interesting thing to you about making records? Is it the putting together of different sounds?
RS: (sigh) That's what I want to know. I don't know exactly what it is.
TS: You starred in *The Last Emperor* and *Merry Christmas Mr. Lawrence,* and wrote the soundtracks as well. I can't think of anybody else who has done that.
RS: Mmmh. Yes.
TS: What does acting give you that music doesn't, both positively and negatively?
RS: Basically I hate acting, and I don't think I'm a good actor. I hate to act a fanatic Japanese. But I love to act a good, naive modern guy. (laughs) On the set I have to wait a long time. I found acting is waiting, and it's boring. But I love to do work with the movie people and the productions, because usually I'm alone in the studio making music. So it's fun to work with a lot of people who come from different areas. For instance, in *The Last Emperor* they came from France, Italy, China, Japan, England, America. So that's really fun.
TS: Has it changed your life, *The Last Emperor?*
RS: Before the film I traveled outside of Japan a lot, so, it's not that different. But I touched the feeling of internationality with this film.
TS: What struck you most about working with Bernardo Bertolucci on *The Last Emperor* set?
RS: I learned how artists should be. I thought Bernardo is like an artist in the 19th century—very egomaniacal, very schizophrenic. He was selfish, and then gentle. Very arrogant, emotional. That's fascinating to me.
TS: You do a lot of commercials for Nissan, Chanel, and so on. Companies come to you and ask you to wear their clothes and put on their sunglasses. Is it only for the big money, or do you enjoy the visibility it gives you?
RS: It's mainly for money. But I enjoy it. Japanese TV commercials are different from American ones. I hate to say it— commercials are commercials—but Japanese commercials are a bit more sophisticated.

TS: You're an idol in Japan. What is your daily life like? Is it crazy? Can you go outside to a restaurant in Tokyo without people following you down the street?

RS: (laughs) No, I can't. I have to change my face to go out.

TS: Do you enjoy being famous?

RS: No.

TS: What is the most beautiful music you ever heard?

RS: That's difficult. From Debussy's *Three Nocturnes* I love the first part, "*Nuages.*" And the second movement of "*La Mer.*" I like *The Last Emperor* too.

TS: Your albums range from classical to jazz to reggae and funk. What kinds of music are you most interested in now?

RS: Now? All kinds except Hawaiian music, and country and western music. (laughs)

TS: Are there other arts that interest you as much as music?

RS: Yeah. I am interested in David Salle, the painter. Robert Longo. And I like David Lynch in films. I love his first film, *Eraserhead.* And another painter, Shinro Otake.

TS: If you had to produce a dream record with famous artists — they can be either alive or dead — do you have any idea who you would choose?

RS: Wow.

TS: Crazy question, isn't it?

RS: Yes. Okay, I would like to use Jimi Hendrix for guitar, maybe Bill Laswell for bass, and maybe Sly Dunbar [on drums], and maybe the horn section from Sly Stone. I could have artists like Coltrane for solo parts. And strings from The Berlin Philharmonic.

TS: Why not? The Berlin strings would be great with Jimi Hendrix.

RS: It would cost money. (laughs)

1988

STOLEN MOMENTS

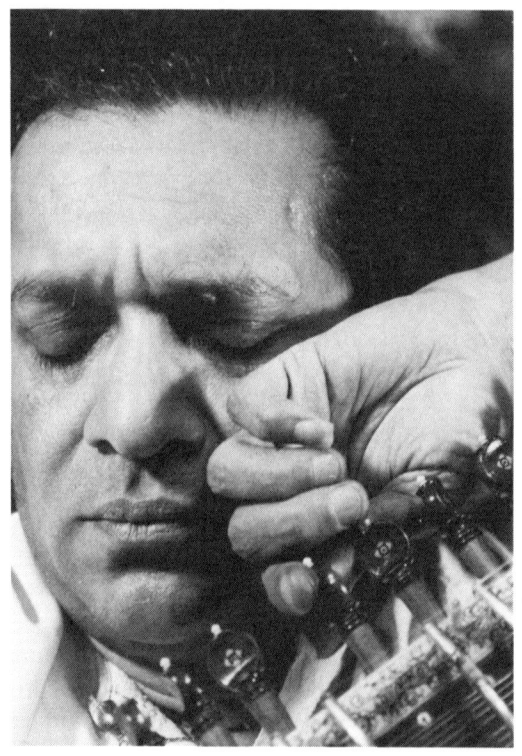

"Can you imagine, after all the best hotels, I had to go and stay in a little room? The heat, the cockroaches, scorpions, snakes..."

RAVI SHANKAR

ONCE GUITARIST JOHN MCLAUGHLIN ASKED AN INDIAN MUSI- *cian friend for Ravi Shankar's address, and he was told simply to write "Ravi Shankar, India." Sure enough, in a while came the reply.*

A celebrated master in his own country, nobody has done more to popularize Indian classical music in the West than Ravi Shankar. While many have heard at least a sampling of his rhapsodic music, few may realize what a remarkable life this peaceful and profound man has had. Our conversation spanned continents and decades, from Harlem to Bangladesh, from earthly pleasures to spirituality.

TS: Ravi, you were born in Benares, one of the oldest and holiest cities in India. What was it like growing up there? Did you have a normal childhood?

RS: Until about ten I suppose I had a normal childhood. I grew up in that very interesting city, the oldest existing city in the world.

TS: How old?

RS: Well, it's mentioned in all our Vedic scriptures. People say about ten thousand years. So it was really fantastic. It's on the bank of the river Ganges, and it's the holiest city for the Hindus. People come from all over India to die there.

TS: It's hard to imagine, being in Los Angeles which is one of the newest towns in the world, that a city could be so old. You first started not as a musician but as a dancer in your older brother's dance company, the Uday Shankar Company.

RS: Right. 1932. When I was twelve I came here with my brother's troupe.

TS: And I guess this company, along with the Anna Pavlova Ballet, were Sol Hurok's biggest acts.

RS: It was. My brother, Uday Shankar, was a partner of Anna Pavlova for a couple of years. He did two ballets based on Indian themes, *Radhakrishna* and *Marriage Ceremony in India*. So this was in the mid-twenties. He had toured all of the States and South America with her. After he left her, he wanted to do something by himself, get musicians and dancers from India and have a troupe. And that's how he came to India. He brought all the three brothers, including me, the youngest, and my mother and my cousin, my uncle and a few other musicians. We went straight from Benares to Paris, which was such a shocking change for me at that age.

I still can remember it vividly. We went by boat, and there was this gradual progression, first seeing the city of Bombay, which was the largest city. From then on I was in a fever with excitement, reaching Paris and having a beautiful house where we lived. The whole ballet was working and creating new dance under my brother's direction. Costumes were being made, hundreds of yards of colorful brocade and different headdresses, ornaments. Then all the musical instruments my brother had collected—150 different varieties, all originally Indian, mostly folk, and lots of classical instruments. So I grew up for the next few years in that atmosphere of dance and music. In Paris I was put into school for about a year and a half, but that ended. I was taught English, mathematics and things like that by my other two brothers. But it was dance and music that I lived in, so that was great.

TS: How did being a dancer affect your music? Were you a

musician then too, or did music come later?

RS: No, simultaneously both together. When I first went to Paris, being small, I couldn't participate in all the dance. There were only special roles, like in the ballet I did the snake demon fighting Lord Krishna, or the part of Hanuman, the monkey god, in an episode of the *Ramayana*. But gradually as I grew up I took dancing more seriously, and I had a solo. Even the great critic John Martin wrote a very good review of my solo which I choreographed myself at the age of sixteen. Musically, you see, it was strange. I could pick up any instrument—sitar, sarod, flute, tabla, whatever I got hold of—and play without any training. This was good and bad at the same time, because anything I was doing people were praising, saying how wonderful I was.

So I was quite spoiled, you know. I thought I was good. But unfortunately I never had any proper training. But this is when the man who became my *guru* later on, Baba Allaudin Khan, father of our famous Ustad Ali Akbar, joined my brother's group as a soloist for one year. This was the end of 1935. He came to Europe and toured all around, starting from Tel Aviv—then it was known as Palestine—Jerusalem, Haifa, and then Greece and Bulgaria and Rumania—the whole of Europe. He went back after one year, but during that year he really changed my life, in the sense that he made me understand that this is a serious thing. He did tell me that I had a lot of talent, but then he said, "What you're doing is stupid. You're not concentrating on one thing, you're doing too many things."

I realized what he was saying but I couldn't help it at that time. He told me, "If you want to learn properly you have to leave all the glitter glamour of this Western world and come to me in my little village where I am living and stay there, and then only I will teach you properly." But he went away and I couldn't leave immediately. I was getting more famous as a dancer and becoming a young man and enjoying myself.

TS: Traveling around the world first class on the *S.S. Normandie*.

RS: Yes, first class. (laughs) Exactly. So it was hard for me. But after some time I felt a tremendous emptiness and I knew that music was the one thing I wanted to do.

TS: Didn't you have a chance to meet people like Gertrude Stein and attend some of her little *soirées*?

RS: From 1930 to 1938, Paris was the main place. We used to tour all over the world, even going to India, but coming back always to Paris. It was our headquarters. Paris was the art capital of the world at that period—all the musicians, dancers, actors, painters, and all the famous expatriates from this country—Gertrude Stein, Cole Porter, Henry Miller. And I distinctly remember there was a dear friend of my brother who was an elderly American gentleman, a good amateur cello player, and his wife. Their house was like a salon. We used to visit there. I remember the name of Gertrude Stein. And of course all the other famous musicians were there—Szigetti the violinist, Heifetz, Pablo Casals . . .

TS: You made your first tour of the United States in the 1930's, if I'm not mistaken. What was that like?

RS: I was so thrilled, because in those days we came by boat, not flying. The very first approach of New York in the early morning through the fog, with the skyscrapers—that's a thrill I think no one can have any more. Today when you come by plane it cannot be the same thing. And the whole country was newer at that time. You know, there was more excitement. Of course there was a lot of ignorance, in the sense that today, with the media, we have become so much more knowing about each other. But at that time there was almost no knowledge about anything alien, any different art form or culture or anything. At that time only my brother, along with Gandhi and Tagore, was known outside India. Uday Shankar was the pioneer in bringing music and dance from India.

TS: Ravi, you said something recently about going to the Cotton Club to see Cab Calloway.

RS: (laughs) Yeah.

TS: So how did you get in? Did you have a fake I.D.?

RS: I don't know how. I was seventeen or so then. I went in fact twice, I think, I liked it so much. It was wonderful, that period in the thirties. The vaudevilles were the famous things, the big cinema houses, apart from the main feature show. They showed cartoons, news, then there was intermission, and there was this hour-long vaudeville show. I saw Eddie Cantor, W.C. Fields, Ed Wynn—all the famous stars of those days.

TS: A lot of people during the depression would go to the show if they could afford it, just to escape the misery of their lives.

RS: I came to the States four times—'32, '34, '36, and 1938. Then came the war and that whole thing helped me to decide. My brother decided to start an institution in the Himalayas called the Shankar India Culture Center. I went back to India and devoted no more time to dance but began learning music from my guru Baba Allaudin Khan. I shaved my head—all the long, curly hair that I had—and gave away all my dresses. Because Baba had been always saying, "You like to dress, you are a dandy. You have to be simple in life, celibate." All those things he used to tell me. I wanted to please him. So I took completely coarse clothes and went to him. He was shocked to see me like that. At the same time I knew this little play-acting pleased him.

But while trying to please him I got into it, little by little. It was very difficult in the initial stage. Can you imagine, after all the best hotels I had to go and stay in a little room? The heat, the cockroaches, mosquitoes, flies, scorpions, the snakes all around. And the hard, coarse bed that I had. So it was a torture for me in a way, physically and also mentally. I used to miss so many wonderful things that I had tasted in my life. It took me about six months to almost one year to get into that. But then under his wonderful, strict but loving guidance, I stayed there for almost seven and a half years, and worked up to fourteen hours a day in some periods. So it was a completely different life and I'm glad that I chose that life.

TS: What was involved in your study of classical Indian music?

RS: Well, he belonged to a very old, traditional school, like the way of teaching religion or yoga. He was not like most of the other musicians. He had strong principles, and was against drinking or drugs. Also he insisted on celibacy in the period of training and learning. So after all these years of total freedom and having all the fun that one can think of, for me to go all of a sudden to such a different atmosphere was difficult in the beginning. But I wanted so much to learn the music and our old ways and our old culture.

TS: One can trace classical Indian music back to the 15th century, I understand.

RS: Yes. Before that we know what happened but we don't have dates. We have old books, scriptures by which our musicologists are finding out a lot of things now. When I was taught, I was given very clear definitions that this was the style as it was done in this period and this period and this period. We learn it orally, and that's how we pass it down.

TS: There was a man named Tansen in the 16th century who I understand was a Bach-type figure. He had a whole new system and was criticized, yet he laid the foundation for modern Indian classical music.

RS: Right. He was in the early 16th century, a very great musician, a singer actually. He was also a yogi. He had his training from a great yogi musician who never came to any palaces. Tansen embodied both vocal power and yogic training, so his music had some sort of miraculous effect. He could bring down rains, or cure people—fantastic, miraculous things. It was not just the music. He had tremendous occult, yogic power.

TS: In Indian classical music there are seventy two full octave parent scales, with twenty two intervals per octave. So we're talking about a lot of quarter tones, which sound somewhat foreign to Western ears at first listening. But with more listening one can perceive the incredible rhythmic and melodic structure.

RS: Especially the rhythmic side has influenced many musicians in the West, because you have such complex and sophisticated rhythmic development.

TS: Ravi, have you finally been able to elude the pop image that was thrust upon you in the sixties?

RS: You know, it just happened. I had to go through that phase. George Harrison of the Beatles became my student, and naturally it created a big star explosion. That was the period of the hippies and the flower children. I think it was good in a way because it brought all the young people to our music. Of course it was a fad, very superficial. That's the negative side of it, the drugs and all that sort of thing. On the other hand, I think what came out of it was good. There were some who stayed out of all that and showed much more respect for our music. They understood much more, and they are the best listeners today.

TS: Is it not true that you inspired George Harrison to produce the Bangladesh Concert in 1971?

RS: That's true. I was going to do it single-handed, myself. But then I thought it wouldn't have that effect. And George happened to be in town at that time. I asked him and he was very willing. Immediately Bob Dylan and Eric Clapton and many other very well known musicians agreed to participate, and it became a great success.

TS: People know about George Harrison. But another great figure studied with you as well, John Coltrane.

RS: Yes, he did. He was a wonderful person. I always remember him. It's a pity that he died so young. He had so much to give. He was one person who was not copying our music but was trying to take the soul, or the inner feeling, which was rather unusual.

TS: He also took the concept of modal improvisation.

RS: Yeah, modal improvisation and drone, of course, was the superficial part. But I think he went deeper that that. That's why he was very anxious to learn more. He came to me and we spent some time together for a couple of months. But he died at that time.

TS: Did you know Mahatma Gandhi?

RS: I met him twice, actually, in two different places in Bombay. It was a wonderful situation. I went along with my brother. He asked me and our group to sing some *bhajans*, religious songs, for him. He was not a person who looked great—very ordinary, frail looking, an old man with almost no teeth. No personality, in the sense that we think of as charisma. But he emitted such a radiance. Of course, knowing who he was made all the difference. If no one told you who he was, no one would look at him twice. But he had tremendous inner strength.

TS: Did you think that the movie *Gandhi* did his legacy justice?

RS: Well, there are people who have criticized it as not being very authentic, not giving enough credit to some people who were with him and very important in his life. But personally, I think the film is wonderful. It gave the gist of Gandhi's life, and it brought out wonderfully his whole message of peace and non-violence.

TS: What is the name of your guru?

RS: Tat Baba was my music guru, and in the spiritual field. But now I'm very much involved with Sai Baba.

TS: This might be a personal question, but if there was anything most important that you've learned from Sai Baba, what would it be?

RS: Well, it's difficult to describe him. He's so different from all other yogis or great spiritual masters. He's known as an incarnation of some very great force. All he teaches is love, compassion. Millions of people have visited him from all over the world. Many give him big credit for being able to materialize things, like this diamond ring.

TS: I was going to ask you about that.

RS: He materialized it out of nowhere.

TS: There was a rumor that a year later you saw Sai Baba again and he apologized, saying, "I'm sorry that it's too small," and re-sized it just by putting it into his hand and giving it back to you.

RS: That's true.

TS: Could you please tell us what happened?

RS: Well, (sighs) it has become such a natural thing to see him do that. He does that so many times every day, giving people rings, necklaces, earrings. He can produce anything from his hand like that—both diamond rings you see I'm wearing. This one that was changed I had had to wear on this finger because it was loose. He just took it and changed it.

TS: Just by blowing on it.

RS: Yeah, and this one he gave me two years ago, with an emerald in between two diamonds.

TS: He conjured them up just by willing them.

RS: Right, but that is not the main thing. It is just one of the little graces of whatever magical thing he does. This is not the point. It is the fact that he gets so much love to be able to attract thousands of people, sitting down in a remote place in India, any day of the year. Look at their faces. They look at him with love, surrendering themselves. That alone shows the very unusual power this person has.

TS: There are many limitations in Western science and Western methods of looking at things.

RS: Exactly. There are nuclear physicists, doctors, eminent scientists who went to him, not believing it, and since then they have become his devotees. From all over the world people are there.

TS: Does he ever come to the United States?

RS: No, he doesn't want to come out here because here he would be treated like a freak. Anyone who wants to see him has to go to India.

TS: You spoke a little bit earlier about your meeting with Mahatma Gandhi. I know Gandhi was once asked what he thought of Western civilization, and he replies that he thought it would be a good idea. (laughs) Do you sometimes think about the superpowers—America, Russia, and the arms race—and the sort of interminable, inexorable struggle to attain even a semblance of world peace? Do you think that's possible, or likely?

RS: Well, like any thinking person I feel scared, with all the pollution and fear of nuclear holocaust. In fact, I have written a few pieces that have not been brought out here but in India, taking this theme. I'm very much worried, especially by the pollution I see. Forget the West—even in India right now. It's so terrible in the lost cities like Calcutta, Bombay or Delhi, so much air pollution it's difficult to breathe. We are very concerned about that. And the superpowers' fearful threats of war and violence seem horrifying and silly.

1988

"John Coltrane demonstrated to me that nothing would shake or deter him from his mission or goal."

WAYNE SHORTER

AMONG THE MOST PROGRESSIVE BANDS TO EMERGE IN THE 1970's was Weather Report, co-founded by Wayne Shorter and Joe Zawinul. A gifted composer and saxophonist, Shorter had already contributed significantly to the work of another great artist, Miles Davis. Personally, he always had a reputation for reclusiveness, inscrutability.

Wayne Shorter once made an album called The Odyssey of Iska, describing Iska as "the wind which comes and goes, leaving no trace." His music always struck me in this same mysterious way. So it didn't surprise me that Shorter in person was quiet and reserved, but always thoughtful in his replies; I enjoyed the challenge of trying to bring him out.

> TS: Wayne, you've won innumerable critic's polls here and abroad. You've played with the greatest jazz bands in modern history—Art Blakey, Horace Silver, Miles Davis, not to mention Weather Report. Wayne Shorter compositions are generally adored by other musicians. Many people have recorded your tunes. In spite of this recognition, you remain

shrouded in mystery to a certain extent. People found the electronics of Weather Report increasingly dense. It seemed a lot of people wanted to see you on your own.

WS: I have a lot of compositions and music that have to do with certain experiences throughout my life—more recently, to be exact. These compositions will be sort of a storytelling vehicle, which I'm going to put out in the world. I'm only going to put out the ones that have the storytelling characteristics. I'm staying away from all the technical acrobatics musicians usually go through in their earlier years.

TS: What was your childhood like? Were you shy or extroverted?

WS: A real introvert. I stayed indoors. When the other kids said, "Come out and play," I would stay inside and draw, work with my hands, with clay. My brother did the same thing. We would create an adventure in the house.

TS: Was it an interior world that you preferred to mingling, or was it just being afraid?

WS: We would make these people on the round kitchen table. We made characters out of the comic strips, the Frankenstein movies. We tried to make World War II. We had the Red army, the Blue army—red clay, blue clay, the brown clay for the American soldiers. We dunked the submarines in the water—the whole thing. One time we tried to make the whole world.

TS: Is it true that you wanted to play the saxophone because it was shiny?

WS: Yeah, it was shiny. But before that the clarinet, the silver keys. That's shiny. Also the ebony, that's shiny too. The trumpet was shiny. The clarinet looked mysterious. But the saxophone was in the middle of serious and something kind of flamboyant.

TS: Did you play in high school?

WS: The last year in high school, because I majored in Fine Arts. I minored in music.

TS: Do you still paint or draw?

WS: Now that I have more time for my own projects I plan to paint and draw a lot more.

TS: How is painting similar to music?

WS: Well, improvisation you do with a band, painting is total solo. In painting, you're really out there all by yourself. People from the inner world come to join you. Fantasy.

TS: You were with Art Blakey, then you went to play with Miles Davis. How did that happen? I understand you had a chance to join Miles Davis after John Coltrane left the band but you turned it down.

WS: I was still with Art Blakey, so I didn't want to leave The Messengers. Why leave a ship? Mutiny, AWOL, desertion. When word gets around that one musician leaves a band for another, there's an immediate phone call. I was thinking about Benedict Arnold and all that. But after that, more time passed and Miles called me at a rehearsal. Art Blakey picked up the phone and Miles said he wanted to speak to me, so we had to stop rehearsal. It was right after that that I joined.

TS: You spent six or seven years with Miles. I imagine you learned a lot. Is there anything in particular?

WS: Miles always picked musicians who had a lot of independence. We all developed even more independence. Not from each other—it went together in a teamwork fashion—but musical independence. We made a lot of records where we played soft, and the volume was down. That kind of thing—respect for the sound coming from the person next to you. That's a highlight.

TS: Do you think Miles learned anything from you? A lot of the compositions on his albums were written by you. Would he ask you for things?

WS: Well, he would call and say (imitating Miles's whisper) "What do you have?" (laughs) And I'd say, "Well, I have about three things I've been working on." Then he would call Herbie, and Herbie would have maybe one or two. But beyond that, anything Miles learned he kept to himself.

TS: John Coltrane was more than just a musician, he was a spiritual giant for many. Did he give something that inspired you as a musician?

WS: Yes. The overall something that he demonstrated to me was like a bombardment of light. In the night clubs, the talking stopped when he and Elvin really started to deal on the bandstand. He would concentrate, and nothing would shake or deter him from his mission or goal. And the goal, it seemed to me, was like a drama, but also some kind of enlightenment through music. So the evenness and nice flow of his lines were not disturbed by mundane things and actions.

TS: I understand that you practice Nichiren Shoshu Buddhism. How has that affected your life and your music?

WS: Well, I've been involved in practice twelve years. All through those years, aspects of my life other than music have started to come to the surface, things that I needed to do or take care of from years ago—from childhood, from birth. They are becoming more manifest now. The times when people are yelling, "We want to hear more compositions from Wayne!", the music part of my life, was in a state of animated suspension. Other aspects of my life in conjunction with other people's lives have been coming out. A lot of people before they die probably think, "I wish I had taken care of this. I wish I had known my daughter more." It struck me when one of the presidents of CBS walked out. They asked him, "Why?" He said, "My daughter needs me." He gave up his position. So that's an example. These things are very real, not just ethereal.

TS: What if you were stranded on an island with a solar powered record player? What records would you choose?

WS: Did you see *Death In Venice?* The Gustav Mahler? That emotional piece.

TS: I know the piece.

WS: And I'd like something by Yma Sumac. Stravinsky's *Rite of Spring,* and *Song of the Nightingale.* And a string of Bud Powell records, from the early days. And some of those out-takes from Charlie Parker that they're starting to make into "in-takes" slowly. And I'd like a lot of good top-notch *flamenco.* And some Portugese *fado.* A lot of people don't know what the *fado* is, but when you go to Portugal you will hear it. And some music from a Romanian, Zamfir, playing the pan flute. And some of Africa's best drummers! I'd like, if possible, to have some music from another planet which is

hustling and bustling with living things.
TS: Maybe we can find out about that before our time is up here on earth. Who knows?
WS: Let's hope so.

1987

STOLEN MOMENTS

*"Knowing what I know now,
I would never have gotten
into show business. I would have
picked potatoes, I would have
pleaded with my mom and dad . . ."*

NINA SIMONE

N INA SIMONE HAS A WAY OF CONVINCING YOU. HER SONGS, *like Billie Holiday's, penetrate to the core with their simple honesty. Her voice is rough and sounds as if it's coming through dark velvet; her range is only an octave and a half or so, but she makes every note count. She can be a fiery performer, her angry voice backed by a flurry of well-articulated piano notes; or she can cripple you with a simple song of lost love, and chords of pristine, Bach-like delicacy. Her Town Hall concert of September, 1959 is surely one of the most beautiful set of songs ever recorded.*

Sadly, many of her great records are unavailable. Her recordings have tended to be sporadic, separated by as much as a decade. Nina Simone is both diva *and naive Little Girl Blue, as adored by her fans here and in Europe as she is avoided by managers, agents, and club owners who fear her mercurial personality.*

TS: You were a child prodigy, weren't you?
NS: Yes, at three years old I had perfect pitch, and very few of us in the world are blessed with that. That's a gift from God. My little feet could not reach the floor, and I was playing a song

called "God Be With You Till We Meet Again," and I didn't know how I knew it. I had never seen the music. I didn't really know what music was, in terms of written notes. But I knew that song and I knew it was in the key of F.

TS: You grew up in North Carolina, and you had two mothers. One only wanted you to hear spirituals and gospels, and the other one was a woman named Muriel Massanovich.

NS: I started studying classical music with Mrs. Massanovitch, and the first ambition was that I would become the world's first black classical pianist. The only one we have is Andre Watts, and the black world doesn't really accept him. So I was trained to be that from the time I was five or six. Then I was turned down for a scholarship at Curtis Institute. I didn't make it, and it was because of prejudice. I wasn't prepared for that. At that point I had to go into show business to help support my family.

TS: You then took a job at Harry Steward's Midtown Bar in Atlantic City. Was that an abrupt disillusionment when all of a sudden, after your classical studies, you had to sing in a bar?

NS: Oh, yes, it was. I never quite got over it.

TS: You have an album with a curious title, *Fodder on my Wings*. What does that mean?

NS: I wrote the song *Fodder on my Wings* on the balcony of my Swiss apartment. One night I had slept quite deeply and I woke up and I looked down on civilization and I saw the order of the children going to school. I saw the silence and everyone doing the same thing the same way at the same time. And I said, "What on earth am I doing here?" I remembered the concrete that housed the place where I stayed—it was a highrise. Then the word came to me, it's "fodder." I said, "Fodder?" I went to my dictionary and hurriedly found the word. I found out that it meant manure, hay, something that you used for cattle to eat and to lie in for comfort. Then I remembered I knew that I was a reincarnated entity. So the words to the song are that of a small bird who fell here to this planet. And she only fell because one of her wings was crippled. She fell in the country, in this fodder. She's a delicate, delicate bird. Because she was crippled, she couldn't fly, but she had a third eye and could see all people everywhere. She would try to get out of the fodder, flying from country to country when she had the strength.

TS: Are there any particular artists or people who inspired you?

NS: Yes, I love Ray Charles, Lena Horne. Duke Ellington, of course. John Coltrane, Dizzy Gillespie, Miles Davis. Not many women singers.

TS: Are there any classical pianists who give you the same spiritual depth or nourishment as these other musicians?

NS: Yes, Rubinstein. I listen to him every morning. And Alexander Brailowsky from Juilliard. And Vladimir Horowitz, the greatest technician there is. These guys give me a lot of spiritual nourishment.

TS: On a musical level and on a spiritual level we're talking about the same thing, aren't we? I see nothing strange about playing John Coltrane next to Mahler or Rubinstein.

NS: Yes, Coltrane, my god, yes.

TS: Did you ever have a chance to meet John Coltrane?

NS: Yes, I not only met him, I was privileged to give him a book of poetry by Langston Hughes called "Simple." And I kissed his cheek one time and it was the softest I'd ever kissed in my life. I'll never forget it. It was before he passed away. I was privileged to do that.

TS: Nina, you have called your musical ability both a gift and a burden.

NS: Well, when you're given a gift it is your duty to give it back to the world. If you are humble, and I like to think that I have been, you develop this craft and you give it back to the world. The burden part is that everyone expects you to know everything about everything. And they never stop wanting.

In retrospect, knowing what I know now, Tom, I would never have gotten into show business. I would have picked potatoes, I would have pleaded with my mom and dad. I would have done anything to continue my classical studies. Oh, no, no, no, this was a mistake. (laughs) I'm stuck with it now. I serve God with my music and I'm very, very happy to be given these gifts. But as far as I'm concerned, my being a human being and an imperfect human being has made me unequipped to deal with the talent that God gave me, because I mean it, that if I had my choice... (Nina begins to cry)... I would never have gotten into (whispering) show business.

TS: Obviously the gift and the burden is still there.

NS: That's why I'm going to Egypt to finish my autobiography.

TS: Your public is an adoring, faithful, but very jealous lover, too, isn't it?

NS: (quietly, still crying) Yes, very.

TS: You want to go back to music for a minute, Nina, or you want to keep talking?

NS: Sure.

TS: I know your fans . . . well, "loyal following" is not really strong enough, the way your fans feel about you and the way that you communicate with them. You must feel a psychic thing happening when you perform because the people know the words. I suppose they're the best friends you have.

NS: That's right. Those of you who are my fans, I know you are somewhat (sighs heavily) disgusted and probably confused as to why we have not bought the whole cult—for lack of a better word, "cult," because I'm not really religious in the way we should be, that other people are. I know that you are confused about why I haven't brought all of you together and housed you in some little place where you could worship together in peace. I'm not sure why I haven't either, except I'm afraid. If I get enough bodyguards, I perhaps may do that. That's for your ears, and don't forget that I at least said it, after four decades in the music business, on KCRW this morning. I simply do not have enough protection in my personal life to take that chance.

1987

NICOLAS SLONIMSKY

NICOLAS SLONIMSKY IS THE SORT OF PERSON YOU MEET ONCE *in a lifetime. At 94, he still has the impish look of a clever child, immensely pleased with himself. Although a composer of both serious music and outrageous radio commercials, and a conductor of major 20th century premieres by Charles Ives and Edgar Varèse, he still considers himself a "failed* wunderkind." *He's worked with musicians from Stravinsky to Zappa, and Oxford University Press recently published his autobiography,* Perfect Pitch, *which Leonard Bernstein characterizes as an* "Encyclopaedia Brittanica *of music written by Oscar Wilde."*

Slonimsky showed up for our hour together with piano-key suspenders and a fish tie. He also brought along an orange and a lint brush with which he performed two of his études. And he indulged in one of his favorite pastimes: playing piano facing backwards, which he calls "retrodigital tergiversations."

TS: Nicolas Slonimsky, welcome.

NS: It's wonderful to be allowed to talk endlessly, because you see unless I'm stopped I will go automatically, because I

"Zappa began with Edgar Varèse and became a great promoter of Varèse's music. Fortunately Varèse had died before he knew about Frank Zappa's..."

suffer from a curious ailment which is known as *logoria*. Now *logos* means word and *ria* is the same as diarrhea. So the incontinence of words is logoria. Here is my contribution to etymology.

TS: (laughs) I'm happy to have you here, logoria and all. You were born in St. Petersburg, in 1894? Is that correct?

NS: Yes. Now, I usually introduce myself by saying that I was born in a town that changed it's name twice to exorcise the stigma of being my birthplace. You see, it became Petrograd in 1914 when Russia went to war with Germany. Of course they couldn't have a German name for their capital, so they changed it to Petrograd, which is the translation. *Grad* means town in Russian, and *Petro* of Peter the Great who did found this place. Then Lenin died in 1924, and his associates decided to celebrate his name rather than Peter the Great's name. So it became Lenin the Great and so it's now Leningrad. So I was born in St. Petersburg. I left Petrograd. I revisited Leningrad.

TS: What were your first musical experiences? I understand you spent some time living in Scriabin's house.

NS: Well, that was much later when I was already grown. But my first experience was to listen to my celebrated aunt. Her name was Isabelle Vengerova. She became a piano teacher at the Curtis Institute of Music, and among her students were Leonard Bernstein and Lukas Foss, Samuel Barber and many others. She became sort of a celebrity in the United States after she had a complete career as a pianist and teacher in Russia. She was my mother's sister and so naturally she would practice in our house. She used our piano and I listened to all the wonderful sounds.

That was my first impression of music. Then I discovered, or rather my admiring relatives discovered, that I had the gift of perfect pitch, which means that I could play any kind of note that was played on the piano or whistled or played on the harmonica or anything. So my mother informed me that I was a genius. I was six years old, and I decided that geniuses don't have to practice, so I stopped practicing. That's the sad story of my early years.

TS: I understand that as an adolescent you wrote your future biography and listed your date of death as 1967.

NS: Well, it looked like it to me, when I wrote my autobiography in 1910, you see, fresh after watching Halley's Comet. In St. Petersburg that comet hung over the river. It was as big as Venus, or even bigger than Venus. No, I did not die in 1967, because I had to finish my dictionary and start my autobiography. So I cancelled that date and decided to live on until 2001.

TS: What were you doing during the Russian Revolution? Where were you?

NS: I was in Petrograd. That was 1917.

TS: What were things like there?

NS: Things were cold. There was no food. There was no entertainment, and the streets were impassable. There were icebergs all over the place. It was, in fact, the coldest winter since Napoleon's invasion of Russia in 1812, and the second coldest going forward to 1941, when the Nazis attacked Russia. The Nazis were not used to that kind of weather.

TS: Were you aware that what was happening would change the face of Russia forever?

NS: I certainly was aware, because I was born in an intelligentsia family, which was full of revolution, mostly verbal revolution. None of my family could handle any kind of weapon, and neither could I. But we were all full of revolution against the oppression of the czars and so forth. Of course we didn't realize what was coming up, the situation by which the czar would appear just a babe in the woods, so ineffective, liberal in a way in comparison with what happened after that.

TS: Did you hear about the 1913 Paris premiere of *The Rite of Spring* as a young music student?

NS: Well, I wasn't in Paris. Stravinsky was an unknown quantity in Russia and in fact his teachers were not particularly fond of his type of music. The director of the St. Petersburg Conservatory, the revered Glazunov, when he was asked about Stravinsky, said, "No talent whatsoever, just dissonances." So I didn't know much about what was going on in Paris, because Paris was beyond our conceptual limits. We knew that there was modern music and we knew that Scriabin could compose music that began with a dissonance and ended with a dissonance.

But it was nothing in comparison with Stravinsky's *Le Sacre du Printemps*. When I finally emigrated and went to Paris, of course I realized that *Le Sacre du Printemps* was a momentous work. The music still affected me as being a very strange piece to compose because it didn't sound like Tchaikovsky at all. And Tchaikovsky to me was the model to imitate. In fact, I did imitate Tchaikovsky as best—or worst—as I could in my own compositions. Then I began imitating Rachmaninoff. Then I began imitating Scriabin, and then I said, "Oh what the hell, let me imitate myself."

TS: Now I've heard different people talk about these little jingles you wrote in the thirties, before radio advertising was developed. What were they?

NS: Well, I have a claim to be the first person who wrote commercial jingles. They were not very marketable. And when I proposed them to various manufacturers of products whose manufacture I extolled in my very emotional pieces, one of those manufacturers threatened to sue me if I would try to perform them. Apparently they realized that I was not composing commercial jingles but I was making fun of their advertising copy.

TS: You did one for a linen company?

NS: Yes, that was all right, Utica sheets and pillow cases. That was very emotional, in the style of Schubert.

TS: Pillsbury bran muffins.

NS: Yes, that was a laxative advertisement.

TS: And the Castoria ad? [For a baby's castor oil.]

NS: That's my favorite. It is a work that I called my peristaltic work. I don't know whether peristaltic is in your vocabulary. I hope it can be mentioned on a live broadcast.

TS: Yes, peristalsis. Basic factor in daily life.

NS: That is what Castoria is supposed to produce. And this was the only company that allowed me to use the word to compose this music. It was very emotional, starting with the appeal: "Children cry for Castoria," and then an even more emotional appeal: "Mothers, relieve your constipated child!" That's the height of my work.

TS: I understand that Serge Koussevitzky came to Paris in the early twenties and you followed him in 1923. You describe yourself as having been Koussevitzky's secretary and piano pounder.

NS: That's right, that's what I did.

TS: Now my spies told me that Koussevitzky had a hard time reading scores and you had to help him read *The Rite of Spring*.

NS: Well, this has been one of those legends that I have been trying to deny for the last sixty years. But it's still undeniable. I had a lot of trouble with Koussevitzky because he praised me beyond measure. Whenever he would meet someone he would say that he had a helper who was a mathematician, who was a genius at calculations, who could add fractions, which he couldn't. In other words he behaved as a landed lord who praised his serfs. You know, at that time serfs were measured by their skills. There were advertisements in the Russian papers 150 years ago—"Serf for sale. He is a good barber and he can also play the clarinet." Now this was me. I couldn't play the clarinet, but I played the piano.

TS: Can you recall a typical Koussevitzky rehearsal? What was he like, without using any four letter words?

NS: You see, there are no four letter words in Russian. They are all thirteen letter words. (laughs) But Koussevitzky's rehearsals were very funny, because he didn't speak any foreign languages. He spoke languages that he believed were foreign languages but they weren't.

TS: You were fired for insubordination?

NS: That's right. Where did you get that? (indignant)

TS: Why did he fire you?

NS: Well, my crime was that I was not following his instructions, and furthermore, I was impertinent. See, I was telling him off. And that was certainly a crime. So he fired me and he was right, I was wrong. Because you don't talk to the boss that way. He would ask me was there anything wrong during the rehearsal and I would say the double bassoon played F-sharp instead of F-natural in the seventh bar of the introduction to . . . I don't know what.

TS: Okay, perfect pitch.

NS: Perfect pitch and everything else, and also perfect ability to surmise what the right note was to be. So Koussevitzky didn't like it even though he praised me—but he praised me as a property.

TS: I see. Nicolas, you've written a number of "minitudes," correct?

NS: Yes, they are minitudes, not miniatures or anything like that. They're very short, and that is their only claim for popularity. They are so short that a person has no time to express any dissatisfaction with them.

TS: You created an orchestra to perform premieres, did you not?

NS: Well, I sort of assembled that orchestra because they have to be specially trained. You mustn't forget it was over fifty years ago, and orchestral musicians were not accustomed to this type of wild music. Now *Ionization* by Varèse, which I premiered, is dedicated to me, because no one else would play it. I was the only one who volunteered to play it. And it is written for percussion only, plus two sirens. They had to be manual sirens from the New York Fire Department. Varèse had a hell of a time getting them from the fire department. We couldn't even broadcast a piece because only the fire department was allowed to broadcast any sirens. So it was quite a thing.

TS: Frank Zappa has always extolled the virtues of Varèse's music, hasn't he?

NS: Actually, Frank Zappa told me that he learned to compose by examining and studying scores by Edgar Varèse, which surprised me very much because Varèse composed music of the highest complexity. And here was Frank Zappa, who was supposed to come from the depths of rock and roll, studying this kind of thing. But you see, the extremes always meet. So Frank Zappa and Varèse were like the south pole and north pole of music. Zappa had no schooling. He began with Edgar Varèse and he became a great promoter of Varèse's music. Fortunately Varèse had died before he knew about Frank

Zappa's.
TS: Have you listened to The Mothers of Invention?
NS: Oh, yes.
TS: And what do you think?
NS: Well, I became quite a buddy of Frank Zappa's, sort of an unnatural friendship, but I liked it very much. Of course, he studied my book *Thesaurus of Scales and Melodic Patterns,* which is a sort of compendium of all possible and impossible progressions of tones.
TS: I understand when that was given to a computer, it took the computer fifteen days to figure it out, is that right?
NS: Well, that's a slight exaggeration, but that's all right. I like exaggeration because it sort of rebounds to my fame or infamy or whatever I represent. But a German computer took about two and a half hours to figure out one particular spot in my thesaurus, in which I tried to combine twelve different notes of the chromatic scale in four different triads. And that's quite a trick and I will not go into details because then people will simply tune off our broadcast if I started that.
TS: John Coltrane was also a student of that book.
NS: Yes, how did you know that? I didn't boast to you about it. I found out about it after John Coltrane's death. He discovered my book a few years after publication, and he told his musicians to scrap all of their music books and start studying this. This is true, I found this out from his assistants after he was already dead. So that made me famous in an unexpected slice of humanity.
TS: The next subject, Nicolas, is Charles Ives.
NS: It is a sort of fantastic tale of a genius who was not only not recognized, but was not even noticed as an existent composer and who didn't care about it because he had funds. He actually was an insurance salesman.
TS: Working for the Hartford Insurance Company.
NS: Yes. And he did very well so he didn't have to earn a living with his music. But he was an educated musician. It is wrong to classify him as a wonderful amateur who had genius but no technique. He was a graduate of the music department at

Yale University under Horatio Parker, who was a German-trained musician, and the early works of Ives sounded like either Scriabin or Dvořák. But in his later works he established something absolutely new, a union of American songs—including hymns because he was an organist, a church organist—and tremendous involvements of modern combinations and dissonances that were not even known at the time Ives composed his music. Then at the age of forty-four, in 1918, Ives suffered a heart attack and practically stopped composing music. All of his production can be timed before 1918.

TS: And yet his works were usually not performed until far later. Correct? No one would touch them.

NS: No one would touch them because he was regarded as an amateur who tried to do something different but didn't really know harmony and counterpoint. This is not true. He knew his harmony and counterpoint very well, except he produced something entirely new. And I must say that my most prideful accomplishment was that I realized when I met him and examined his score that there was a genius at work. So I was the first to perform his greatest work, perhaps, *Three Places in New England,* which I conducted at my concert on January 10th, 1931 in New York. And Ives was present. I believe this was the only time he attended any concert when he heard any of his works, because he was a recluse. He didn't have a radio. he didn't have a phonograph, he never read newspapers. He was that kind of a fantastic individual.

And so my friendship with Ives was quite extraordinary because after all, I had just come out of Russia and he was a composer who was quintessentially American. Yet we found some way of harmonizing our philosophies of music.

TS: You were friends with Henry Cowell. He was sort of victimized, wasn't he?

NS: Yes, well Henry Cowell was a great friend of mine, and I was the first to conduct "Synchrony" in Berlin with the Berlin Philharmonic in February, 1932. Now, note that it was 1932. I couldn't have conducted it in 1933 because something happened in Germany in 1933 which was not conducive to my career or the career of Henry Cowell.

Now, Henry Cowell was victimized for two reasons. The first is that he was a "red." You know, he wasn't really a communist or anything, but he was an extreme liberal and contributed to liberal magazines and was the first American composer who actually went to Russia in 1928, when Russia was, of course, an "evil empire." Yet Henry Cowell was very interested in the experimental music that was produced in Russia, so he went. And that was bad.

Then he was rumored—as I say, rumored—to be, shall I say, unconventional in his sexual orientation. Nowadays, of course, anything goes. But at the time, despite the fact that it was in San Francisco, which was very advanced in all kinds of things, he was railroaded into prison because it was found that he allowed some kids to use his car.

Anyway, the Hearst papers got after him and advertised him as the Oscar Wilde of California. Finally he was arrested, even though he wasn't in California—he was in Europe when the alleged offense occurred. But the police got hold of some kids who testified against Cowell in order to save their own skins. If there was any truth in this accusation, nobody could find out. Cowell had to plead guilty in order to save the situation, and he was promised privately that he would be put in a sanitarium for a few months and that would be all. Instead, he was given three to fifteen, and sent to San Quentin.

Well, that was about 1938. He stayed in prison for three and a half years. Fortunately he was released when everyone testified in his favor, and he married a remarkable woman who is still alive, Sydney Cowell. And he continued to compose. He wrote sixteen symphonies altogether.

TS: Nicolas, I guess your most popular book is *The Lexicon of Musical Invective,* subtitled "Critical Assaults on Composers Since Beethoven's Time." When did that all start? Have you been fascinated with words all your life?

NS: Well, it's not words. It's the changing appreciation of art, music and literature. And since I was connected with the

Boston Symphony Orchestra, as secretary to Serge Koussevitzky, and I occasionally supplied information for the program notes for the Boston Symphony Orchestra, I was amazed at the way great composers were treated at the time of the production of their greatest pieces. And so I began collecting all the wonderful, I mean wonderful reviews—things that I found in old newspapers that would be said about not only Wagner and Berlioz but about Tchaikovsky! What could be sweeter than Tchaikovsky's music? And yet when Tchaikovsky's *Piano Concerto* was produced in Boston, it was considered a wild piece of music no real music lover could ever learn to love. So I gathered all those quotations—it took me some years, from different newspapers—and presented it to the world. It became my bestseller, really.

TS: You have a very interesting chapter at the beginning of your *Lexicon*, "Non-acceptance of the Unfamiliar," which is a perfect way of describing the different reviews from Beethoven's time. Was there a particular review here that you thought was the most outrageous of all?

NS: Well, I like outrageous reviews because they serve my purpose. Perhaps the most favorable review of all was the one I myself got in Berlin in 1932, when I conducted a perfectly innocent piece by Wallingford Riegger. One Berlin reviewer wrote as follows, and I will say it in English of course, but the German original was a work of art in itself. It was outrageous but beautifully written. This is what the writer said: "It sounded as though a pack of rats were being slowly tortured to death. And from time to time a dying cow would moan." It's a very surreal picture, of course. It doesn't correspond to the music, which is completely acceptable, but that's how it was.

TS: We appreciate your *logoria,* Nicolas.

NS: Thank you for enduring it.

1988

STOLEN MOMENTS

"In 1975 I was threatened with death.
But I stayed because I lived, like I do now,
traveling from one place to another..."

MERCEDES SOSA

THROUGHOUT LATIN AMERICA, MERCEDES SOSA IS A GIANT OF the nueva cancion, or "new song" movement that started in the 1960's, championing human rights in the face of government brutality and repression. When she returned from exile to sing Violetta Parra's "Gracias A La Vida" in Buenos Aires a few years ago (an event which fortunately was recorded), you hear in the background the thunderous applause of fifty thousand people.

She appears on stage in a simple peasant dress, accompanied by another guitarist, a bassist, and a percussionist. Her voice, deep and rich, expresses the hopes and dreams of millions.

TS: Was your childhood in Tucuman, Argentina happy?

MS: Yes, because we were with my father, my mother, my brothers and sisters, surrounded by my father's large family. So I didn't just grow up in the city, but also near nature, trees, things that also greatly influence a person's life. Tucuman is both a city and the smallest province of Argentina. It's in the northeast. The entire city depends on the production of sugar. The economy was based on the harvest of sugar cane until 1968, when they closed eleven sugar mills, which affected all the workers who had been employed there for generations. The city survives because they built Scandia truck factories, Grafa tablecloths and sheets. The Japanese built factories. They tried to keep all the manpower that had worked in the mills from leaving the province, find them other work. It's called "the garden of the Republic." Everything blooms there—flowers, trees.

TS: People told you that you had a nice voice as a child, as I understand. Did you dream of becoming a famous singer?

MS: No. I didn't like to sing in public. I am enormously timid, so much so that when I get on stage it takes me three or four songs to overcome it. I've spent my whole life trying to overcome this timidness, to be able to communicate with people, or at least enjoy what I'm singing. The people have guided me to the place of popularity I now occupy. But I never wanted to be a singer either in Tucuman or anywhere else in the world.

TS: Do you enjoy being famous?

MS: No. I enjoy singing on stage or off, for friends, but not this life of hotels, planes, tours that I've done practically since I began my career.

TS: You've been called "the voice of the silent majority." Do you feel that this imposes a huge responsibility on you?

MS: For many years I've known that I have a responsibility to sing for people all over the world, those who supported me and helped me all my life. Young Germans, young Dutch feel that I am almost like a mother to them. They see me also not just as a sweet mother but as one who is frequently rather aggressive on stage. The songs have changed over time, from songs of struggles and of barricades to songs which speak more of the anguish of every human being. When I returned to Argentina in '82-'83, I found out that I had to find a new way to express myself on stage to my people, to give them the encouragement to continue, because the struggle to live in Argentina and in Latin America is hard enough. I didn't want to create more problems for them, but show them a new energy.

TS: Then you now choose to stay away from politics?

MS: Yes. I have every right to my thoughts and ideology off-stage, because off-stage I'm a consumer, a taxpayer, a person just like anyone else. But on stage I'm presenting another kind of energy. It's another agenda. So I don't think there's been such a radical change in Mercedes Sosa that she denies things, but it's another way of singing that has opened many roads all over the world, so that I can talk to people about whatever I want when I'm off-stage without having to sing certain songs on stage to get my message across.

TS: You left Argentina in exile in 1975.

MS: In 1975 I was threatened with death by the AAA [the paramilitary police]. They arrested me with 350 people in La Plata, singing *"Cuando Tenga La Tierra."* ["When the Land is Yours."] But I stayed because I lived, like I do now, traveling from one place to another. It was really a crazy attitude, but undoubtedly it spared my life. Of course I finally had to leave in '79, because I had no work. They took away all my work—radio, television, personal appearances. I was in Paris one year, but in 1980 I had to do a long tour in Brazil, and really it was obvious that I wasn't going to live in Paris. I felt far from home. So I went to Madrid because of the language.

TS: You once said that "We are the people with hot blood and postponed dreams . . . "

MS: Exile is really, like the Greeks said, the most severe punishment you can make a person suffer. A popular singer has to be very strong to stand being so far from the things she sings about. I have been privileged, like very few artists, because during my exile I worked, and people helped me a great deal.

TS: Have you suffered any other great disillusionments in life?

MS: The death of my husband in '78. Everything happened to me at once. In '78 I was permanently prohibited from living in Argentina. One can overcome all these political things. What is very difficult to overcome is the death of loved ones, against which you can do nothing but wait until this great pain subsides.

TS: When you look back over your career is there any one thing that you're most proud of?

MS: Yes. The love of my artist friends, because they helped me, and continue helping me.

TS: Is there anything that you haven't done that you passionately want to do?

MS: Yes. I want to take my granddaughter to the house I have in Madrid, to enjoy two months with her and my son, and to rest a little. I'm going to be 53 years old, which is a lot of years to be singing.

TS: What do you enjoy doing most when you're not singing and traveling?

MS: I like to have friends visit, to talk with friends that I love, to read. Reading for me is something very important. Right now we're lucky enough to have the writer Isabel Allende, the niece of President Allende, who lives in Venezuela. At the moment she is the greatest writer in Latin America. I notice the enormous difference between the European intellectuals, the writers, and the intellectuals from Latin America. It's as though the Latin Americans have this magical realism because everything that happens on this continent has that magical quality to it. Europeans have a much more raw realism. The same continent that produced Jorge Luis Borges has produced writers who are trying to reach his stature in writing prose. We are very proud to count that great writer as part of that distant part of South America which we call Argentina.

(translated by Nan Sheri Lieberman)

1987

RICHARD STOLTZMAN

THOUGH CRITICS MAY HAVE CALLED HIM THE GREATEST CLAS-sical clarinetist in the world, praising his recordings of various concerti *and works with chamber ensembles, for me the special magic of Richard Stoltzman is his sound. There is a sweetness and softness in the smooth, vibrato-less playing on his first crossover album,* Begin Sweet World, *that can transform you emotionally, completely change the mood of your home. I wanted to meet and talk with the man who could make such sound.*

TS: I'm probably like a lot of people. I'm not completely nuts about the clarinet.

RS: I'm not either, to tell you the truth. I think it's that everybody either had a sister or a cousin or somebody who played the clarinet, and they got through a couple of the books and made it into the junior high school band or something, and they can remember the pain of those squeaks. After they finally get into the marching band and they're able to get in free to the football games, I think everybody gives it up.

TS: Branford Marsalis played the clarinet, but he said, "You

STOLEN MOMENTS

"There must be something beyond the chromosomes and the chemicals and the dust and the bones that is transcendent. The music tells us that . . ."

know, I started to play the saxophone in high school because I heard you could get women with the saxophone." (laughs)

RS: I don't know what there is to like about the clarinet. I know that I played Oscar the Grouch on Sesame Street, and he liked the clarinet because it was broken up into five pieces. He thought that was excellent that you could break it up like that, and it would look very dirty and all black. My wife evidently liked the clarinet. She went out with several clarinet players, and picked me. So that was a good reason to play the clarinet as far as I was concerned.

TS: I think the reason why I like your music has something to do with the feeling and the sound. There was a critic who said that it's feeling, not technique, that's your secret.

RS: I think that before people know anything about the artist or what is going to be played, their ear is attracted to the sound, the first few notes. There's an almost unconscious decision whether to go ahead and be attentive or to tune it out. It's the tone that does it, the vibrations of the sounds. I think what I've tried to do with the clarinet is make the tone my own and let the instrument speak that way, rather than through some mind-boggling facility that makes it faster and higher and shorter and louder than anybody else.

TS: You did a lot of albums of clarinet concertos. Then a couple of years ago you did an album called *Begin Sweet World,* which you recorded in upstate New York with a few friends. After a month it sold more copies than all your other records together. Why?

RS: I don't know, except that maybe there aren't that many people who flock to the classical bins of music stores. Also, the albums I'd made before *Begin Sweet World* usually contained perhaps one sonata or one concerto on a side of a record, and that limits the possibilities in terms of airplay. Another thing is that some of the pieces on *Begin Sweet World* I had played for many years with Bill Douglass, a pianist and composer friend of mine. Also I've played many of those pieces with visual images. I think those things add up to bring more people into the music, as compared to a Weber concerto or a Brahms sonata, which are also very valid and beautiful pieces.

TS: Richard, your grandmother tinkled the ivories and your father played the saxophone.

RS: That's right. He loved the big bands too. He never became a professional musician but he was always trying to make his tenor saxophone sound like Coleman Hawkins or Ben Webster or Lester Young.

TS: That big, breathy sound. What made you decide to become a musician?

RS: Probably being surrounded with music and hearing it as such a pleasant part of my parent's activities. It gave them so much pleasure. My mother looked forward so much to singing in the church choir and my dad, it was his release from work—coming home, pulling out the tenor saxophone and just letting go. I think feeling that expression of freedom and relaxation from music drew me to it. I kept thinking, "This must be it. What a wonderful world to be a part of."

TS: Did you dream of becoming a classical musician or a jazz player?

RS: Well, my household wasn't a classical household. My dad pointed me towards Ella Fitzgerald, Frank Sinatra, or the big bands. He'd tell me, "Listen to these people. They're really high-standard musicians." So I had no thought about playing classical music particularly. My teachers always had me play both classical standards and jazz standards. I knew that if I went into music I would probably never make a living, at least according to my father.

So I went to Ohio State to study mathematics. Finally I went to Yale and ended up seriously working on chamber music. But I don't know how people get into radio, for instance. You can listen to radio as a child, but just wanting to be an announcer doesn't get you there. And going to college doesn't either, does it?

TS: No. I think you just have to love music. I think a lot of people have fantasies about wanting to become deejays so they can play exactly what they want, and that there might be other people out there who like it too.

RS: The world is very big. Sometimes when I was studying the clarinet and trying to please each individual teacher and trying to do what each person thought was right, I wasn't finding the reason why I should play the instrument. When I started to play simply because it was speaking to me, I found that there were people who liked what I was saying. And that audience hopefully keeps growing. That's what happened with *Begin Sweet World*. There wasn't an audience, it just touched certain people and they would let you know about it. I still get letters from people saying they had their babies while listening to *Begin Sweet World*.

TS: If you have it on and somebody walks in, all of a sudden they'll will say, "What is that?" (laughs) It makes people stop talking.

RS: Well, that's the greatest compliment you can give music.

TS: Does music have some sort of spiritual meaning in your life?

RS: I think it certainly touches whatever it is that you want to call the spirit. I don't think of music as something that I worship, but as an expression of something in the human domain which points to an irrefutable spirit that we must have. When you listen to sounds that move you, you say to yourself, "Even if I don't believe in this, or I don't believe in that, there must be something beyond the chromosomes and the chemicals and the dust and the bones that is transcendent." The music tells us that. So in that respect I have a spiritual relationship with music.

TS: Which composers move you the most?

RS: Well, I'm moved by the fact that people compose—just the act of bringing into existence something that didn't happen before, taking something from the mind and bringing it onto pieces of paper, or improvising it. Creating the sounds, that's a marvel. Mozart has been my most moving experience. I've played Mozart for moments of special significance—Casals' funeral, for instance. He wanted to have the Mozart *Clarinet Quintet* slow movement played. At other very significant moments people have asked for Mozart to be played. So it's linked in my mind with the most profound kind of meanings. But I find every composition, if you look at it and live with it and start to love it, can move you.

TS: Who are your favorite musicians and singers?
RS: I love the sound and the compositional aesthetic of Wayne Shorter. I like the piano playing of Martha Argerich, and of course Keith Jarrett and Chick Corea. There are lots of younger players coming up too that I find very exciting. It's a full world, luckily, and some people that we've maybe never heard of can inspire us just as much as the superstar.

1987

YMA SUMAC

SOME HAVE CHARGED THAT YMA SUMAC, FIRST KNOWN AS A *troubador of "jungle kitsch" in the 1950's, is more of a phenomenon than a singer; yet no less a musician than Wayne Shorter has told me he would take her music to his desert island along with Stravinsky and Charlie Parker.*

And nobody has disputed Yma Sumac's amazing five-octave range—certainly not the World War II Russian generals who threw medals at her feet at sold-out stadium concerts throughout the Soviet Union. Still, reports persisted that Yma Sumac, the South American songstress, never existed, but was a woman named Amy Camus from Brooklyn. I hope the conversation that follows will finally put these rumors to rest.

TS: Yma Sumac, it's wonderful that you're letting listeners hear you again.

YS: That's the reason I've come back to the United States. I want to make people happy again.

TS: You were born in Peru.

YS: Yes, in a beautiful little town, Itchucan, high up in the

"All the Russian artists showed white pigeons to me and took pictures..."

mountains. Not too high because it's in the north. The south is very high. My parents had a farm over there so I was raised with nature, the beautiful pigeons, the beautiful animals. Then when I was growing they brought me to Lima to continue my studies. My parents put me in the Catholic convent. Then after I finished college my parents told me that I should have some career. And I told them, "Yes, I would like to have a beautiful career." When I was a little girl I loved to write beautiful histories. I wanted to be a writer.

TS: Beautiful pictures and words.

YS: Yes. Then I told them, "But I like so much to sing." My mother said, "Oh, never in your life! You want to sing, you sing here in the house. But never in another place." I said, "Yes, mother, but I love to sing. I want to sing all over the world." I was telling her this when I was nine years old. So in my house I built up a beautiful theater, pretended the curtains, the walls and the books were the people. My parents said, "I think she's a little nuts. So my nana, my servant, said, "No, Yma loves to sing very much. The walls, the curtains, the books, even the animals, are people."

TS: And what did you hear at home?

YS: My father's sisters would sing in the house. So I absorbed the way they were singing since I was a little girl. My father used to play the guitar so beautifully it made me cry always. So I said, "Well, when I grow up I'm going to take my father always to travel with me." But when I told them I wanted to be a professional singer they said, "No, no! That is a terrible sin. My daughter will never sing for the people."

But after a long time I convinced them to let me be a professional. After that I got a wonderful contract from Peru's national radio. Every week we had a program. Then the president of the radio station called my ex-husband one day and said, "We have a long distance call for Yma from Buenos Aires, Argentina." They said, "We want Yma Sumac to come." So after three months I went, with my father, naturally.

In Argentina I had tremendous success. Then we had a big proposition from a United States impresario. We started working in New York, in this famous nightclub, The Blue Angel. One night a very handsome, educated gentleman stood up and said, "I want you to come to Hollywood." He was a very important man with Capitol Records. That was in 1951. I made my first appearance at the Hollywood Bowl. It's something I can't forget.

TS: I have heard many things. One of them is that some of the people in Peru thought that you were a reincarnated spirit of an ancient Indian goddess.

YS: That's what they said, especially the native people from the mountains. They love me very much, the children and all the people. They call me *Mama, Mamita!*

TS: Yma, one of the myths that was launched in your direction was that you didn't really exist. There was a reporter who said that in fact your name was Amy Camus, which is Yma Sumac spelled backwards, that you were from Brooklyn, and that you were a Hollywood creation. That must have been amusing to you and maybe a little upsetting.

YS: No, I wasn't angered. By the way, I met that gentleman a few years ago and he was scared of me. But I said, "Come on, let's talk." I said, "Why did you write that?" He said, "You know, Mrs. Sumac, I wrote that because all the big stars in the United States come from Brooklyn. Are you mad at me?" I said, "No, but I want to tell you I'm a real Peruvian. You can see my accent when I speak English. You can check in Peru." And he said, "Will you forgive me please, Mrs. Sumac?" "Don't worry," I said.

TS: Yma, you must hold a world record for attendance at concerts. I had to take out my calculator to find out how many people were in those sold-out concerts for you in the Lenin Stadium in Moscow, where you performed with the Bolshoi Symphony Orchestra. Something like 40 million people heard you there, which is absolutely staggering.

YS: You see, I was invited by the Russian government for three weeks but I stayed six months because I had a tremendous success. Then I started touring the Soviet Union. They gave me a special jet plane. I was traveling with half of the Bolshoi Orchestra, and two doctors, two nurses and everything to take care of me because over there it was winter time, very cold. But Mr. Khruschev was there at my concert. The great composer Khatchaturian, Shostakovitch, and great ballerinas like Maya Pletsiskaya. I saw beautiful music, wonderful ballets.

TS: I'm trying to get a picture in my mind of what it must be like to walk out on a stage at the Lenin Stadium with eighty thousand people, a packed house, waiting to hear you come on.

YS: Oh, I was scared, but I had a tremendous success. I was so happy. When I was singing, all the Russian artists showed white pigeons to me and they took pictures. In my mind I was remembering the way it was in my country with my little pigeons. And there were the soldiers who fought in the Second World War, throwing their medals for me. I said, "No! Keep that! That belongs to you!" I wanted to cry.

1985

STOLEN MOMENTS

"*I think it is boring just
to stay in one kind of musical landscape.
One wants to have mountains here
and seas there
and deserts there and jungle there . . .*"

TANGERINE DREAM

TANGERINE DREAM ALWAYS STRUCK ME AS A BAUHAUS VERSION *of the Grateful Dead. Christopher Franke, along with Edgar Froese and Peter Baumann, founded Tangerine Dream in Berlin twenty years ago; they have remained one of the world's most unusual and adventurous electronic groups. Their post psychedelic, high-tech brew has been called "technopop," a term that would apply to fellow West Germans Kraftwerk and Klaus Schultze, and Tokyo's Ryuichi Sakamoto. If you've never listened to a Tangerine Dream album, there's a good chance you know their visual, trance-like music for* Sorcerer, Firestarter, Risky Business *and other films.*

TS: Chris, Tangerine Dream started in 1968, so I imagine that the title of the group had something to do with the middle of the psychedelic period.

CF: Well, first of all we decided to have an English name to be international. We always felt ourselves a little cosmopolitan. We never found that it was so great to be German. We were traveling a lot and we don't like borders in any way. So we chose this English name. We very much enjoyed music and were into visuals and surrealistic painting. We picked it up from a Beatles song called "Lucy in the Sky With Diamonds." It deals with tangerine trees and dreams and things. We just picked it up for the beauty of it.

TS: I understand you had early concerts where you performed in total darkness.

CF: Yes, we tried to do all kinds of experiments with the ordinary music and drug and dancing scene. If there wasn't a proper place, we played in planetariums or churches where there's a naturally interesting visual environment, or we played in the dark. You get the idea to go to another space or open some doors for the musical imagination. Today we don't need it because people don't need those tricks anymore.

TS: You seem to get a special kind of effect upon your listeners. How would you describe your music? Trance music?

CF: We don't want to stay at one place. We want to move people from point A to point B. New Age music all the time tries to be relaxed. This sometimes gets cheap, like wallpaper music. On the other hand there is hard rock. People like to be upbeat and aggressive. We want to travel through different scenes. I think it is boring just to stay in one kind of landscape. One wants to have mountains here and seas there and deserts there and jungle there. We go through a lot of different things to get smoothly from one atmosphere to another. The ears of the audience deserve more, and we have new computers and synthesizers which can create much more colorful sounds and shapes.

TS: Where do you think your most enthusiastic audience is?

CF: It's changing. It used to be England, then France created a lot of interest. Then our own country, Germany, woke up and listened to the music. Then it spread out to the Eastern Bloc countries, then the southern countries like Spain and Portugal. Of course parallel to that we created an interest in America, and did concerts and gold records. So there is no typical Tangerine Dream fan.

TS: Do you have an interest in surrealist art?

CF: Yes. We were very interested in Dali's paintings at one time.

Our music could learn from these kind of unreal things, because as you get into these stages of music you get more ideas about life and music in general. Music can help find resolutions to problems creative people have. It can be like painting pictures or writing books or even reading books. So every record is a little story, but interpretation is up to the audience all the time.

TS: One thing that Tangerine Dream has gotten involved with over the years is soundtracks. Does composing soundtracks give you a different perspective?

CF: Yes, it's very interesting for us. Our music always seems to attract directors, since we don't use vocals and we use different moods which are simple to put to film. But then we always have visuals in mind when we create music, so there's a natural relationship. We didn't expect that one day we would be quite a big part of this Hollywood mystery.

TS: Have you had a chance to watch MTV here?

CF: Yes. You are watching, then you get crazy after a while. It's always repetition. It's not easy because sometimes there are excellent videos, but you have to see a lot of rubbish before you find one. We have this thing called "Music Box" in Germany, and we watch sometimes. It's not easy these days to create a video. We always say, "Should we create a video?" Then we say, "No, we don't want to get into this kind of stream." We'll hold it back until we have something to show which is a breakthrough. Maybe we'll never do a video because videos are going down now. People are already tired of it.

TS: Tangerine Dream has been together now for quite a while. I'd like to congratulate you.

CF: Thanks. I guess we are veterans at this point.

1986

STOLEN MOMENTS

(WITH MARTIN SCORCESE)

*"When I met Dexter Gordon
I thought immediately,
'My god, this man will be superb.'
He has a way of moving his hands, like birds . . ."*

BERTRAND TAVERNIER

SUDDENLY MUSICIANS JUST BACK FROM EUROPE WERE BUZZING *about a new film,* Round Midnight. *The French have always been crazy about American jazz, and only a French filmmaker would make a film based upon the life of bebop pianist Bud Powell. Only a gifted* cinéaste *or a crazy person would put jazz musicians in the title roles. I guess Bertrand Tavernier is a bit of both.*

TS: Bertrand, the last three films that you made, Mississippi Blues, Sunday In The Country, and now Round Midnight, were about artists. What made you decide to make Round Midnight?

BT: Love for jazz. Passion for jazz. The feeling that the jazz musician had been never properly treated in movies. I mean, you had a couple of nice films like Young Man With A Horn, which was very well directed by Michael Curtiz. Or I remember a film called Pete Kelly's Blues, directed by Jack Webb, with Teddy Buckner and Lee Marvin, and I think, Peggy Lee. But most of the films were always about the white musician—Tommy Dorsey, Glenn Miller, Benny Goodman.

I'd never seen a really good true film about the jazz musician, the bebop musician. So I wanted to do that, to show my love, my passion. I was moved by the story of their life, the emotion. For me it's not only a film for the jazz aficionado but about creation, which deals with a lot of emotion. You know, George Bernard Shaw said something wonderful: "You don't have the right to consummate happiness without producing some." Jazz musicians have given me so much happiness that I wanted to pay tribute to them, and at the same time show people who do not know that music, its essence. And to do a kind of triple love story, between the musicians and their music, between two men, and between me and those musicians.

TS: The story of *Round Midnight* is based upon the relationship between a graphic artist in Paris named Francis Paudras and the great bebop pianist Bud Powell. Could you tell us a little bit about their friendship?

BT: I met Francis by accident when I was doing the research and he began to tell me about his relationship with Bud. I was so moved that I decided it was a plot for the story line. Francis Paudras worshiped Bud Powell, thought he was a great genius, and was so shocked by the way Bud was exploited by the people around him. So he tried to help him. He took him into his home. He discovered that he had never been taken care of, that he had tuberculosis. For three years he helped Bud so he could work and record again and be happy. I saw that it was a story of friendship, passion, love, which was very much linked to the jazz world. I never hear such kind of stories with rock and roll, maybe because rock and roll people are more in the establishment, whereas the jazz musician was outside.

So I paid Francis for the right to use certain events from his life, telling him that I would not do the Bud Powell story. I wanted to do the story of a saxophone player, a fictional character based upon Bud. But I would try to get the emotion out of his story and capture that on the screen.

TS: I understand that Bud Powell spent the first year living with Francis without even saying a word.

BT: I don't know about a whole year. It could have been ten days without saying anything. But after a while he would only answer to Francis and nobody else. Francis found out that he had been given very dangerous pills. He was unable to speak or react.

TS: Why did you decide to use Dexter Gordon to play the role of Dale Turner in this film? Weren't there people saying, "You can't use jazz musicians to play themselves?"

BT: I found them to be very gifted actors, all of them, from Wayne Shorter to Dexter to Bobby Hutcherson. I have never been convinced by actors pretending to be jazz musicians— Paul Newman or Sidney Poitier trying to pretend to play trombone. When I met Dexter I thought immediately, My god, this man will be superb. He has a way of moving his hands, like birds. And he has a bebop walk. He doesn't walk on the two-beat. He has a third beat every two steps. He was great. And nobody can speak, deliver lines like him. I knew that by taking a jazz musician, it would help me to get the film true, capture the emotion and truth in the dialogue.

At the same time it was intimidating when you have somebody like Dexter Gordon, who always was faithful to his music, who never compromised, who only played what he liked to play. He always played bebop, the music that he loved. When you are working with somebody like him, you have to be honest, you have to be true. In that sense I think he helped the film a lot just by being there.

TS: The person playing Francis Paudras is Francois Clouzot. You paint a picture of him that both attracts us and puts us off. He loves and admires Dale Turner in the film, while being cold and sometimes cruel to his ex-wife. Why do you alienate our sympathies that way?

BT: Because I think it was more interesting to show somebody who was not just a great Boy Scout. I like to show the selfish side of people who want to save the world. I think that makes a character more interesting, more living, more biting, more moving. I wanted to show that you can be lonely, that you can be destroyed by creating, that you can be hurt by worshiping people who create. And I wanted to tell the story of two lonely people who have no roots, no family, helping each other. I felt it was moving and more dramatically interesting than to just show the story of a very nice Frenchman.

TS: How did they get along together on the set?

BT: Very well. They had a tremendous admiration for each other. Francois had to play against Dexter, which is very difficult because Dexter is so pure, so organic. You must not rely on actors' tricks. You must unlearn being an actor. Francois said it was the greatest lesson he ever had in his life. He said Dexter's like a mountain. He wrote me a letter saying that he didn't think he would ever feel such strong emotions as the week he spent playing with Dexter.

TS: In your last film, *Sunday In The Country,* the colors were bright yellows, I recall, oranges and greens. With *Round Midnight* you tried to a get a gray-blue color on the screen similar to the color of cigarette smoke.

BT: Exactly. I wanted the color of midnight, the opposite of *Sunday In The Country.* In fact, somebody said that it's the nocturnal version. I wanted to have a certain range and quality fitting the mood, the emotion in the music. I very much believe that a film is a mixing of light and emotion. So you have to find the right light and the right emotion.

TS: Congratulations on a wonderful and unusual film. It presents the music the way it should be presented.

1986

ANDREAS
VOLLENWEIDER

A N ALBUM BEARING THE CURIOUS TITLE, *BEHIND THE GARDENS,* Behind the Wall, Under the Tree, *arrived at the station in 1981. It sounded like a phrase from Clue, a game I enjoyed when I was a kid: "It was Colonel Mustard, with the lead pipe, in the conservatory!" The music was fresh, and different.*

Since that time Vollenweider's electroacoustic harp music has become phenomenally popular; his U.S. concerts are nearly always sold out. A deeply concerned artist, active in ecological and antinuclear movements in Europe, he shared his thoughts with me in a soft, clear voice.

TS: You play an unusual instrument, the electroacoustic harp. It has a very different sound from the average harp. You've modified it, haven't you?

AV: Yes. First of all, I have my own technique, because I never went to a teacher to learn the instrument. I became addicted to this instrument and grew into playing it. That produces the main difference, because I play with fingernails, so it's more percussive. And I have added a damper to the strings,

STOLEN MOMENTS

*"I have made this kind of music all my life.
I don't see any 'New Age' . . ."*

because usually the harp resonates. The sound almost never stops. I built a damper to be able to play more rhythmically, more physically. I have added a few electronic effect units, but they're not so important. I have a microphone for each string, but that doesn't change the sound so much.

TS: The harp is a very mellifluous instrument, a mythical instrument. The Aeolian harp, the classical harp, is almost a symbol of peace in music, and also of a female principle. There are very few men who play the harp. With these feminine associations of the harp, and the ideas of harmony and nurturing, what was it that attracted you to it?

AV: It was a little less romantic. I was looking for my personal instrument. I grew up in a family of musicians, and there were lots of instruments. I tried out almost every type of instrument. I once saw a small Irish harp in the window of a shop. I went in and started to play and bought it, and became addicted to the instrument. I think for every personality there is an instrument to be found, and I think we should go out and search for it, and never be satisfied with what's next to you, what's in your neighborhood. We should exercise our curiosity, and that's what I did. Much later, when I was already playing it for some time, I found out about its history and its background, and it was almost a shock how well it fitted with my beliefs and hopes. It became like a part of my body.

TS: It sounds like when you found this instrument you were able to give expression to things inside that you weren't able to express before. What were those things?

AV: That's difficult to answer, because these things have grown with me all my life. I don't think it's the moment to unfold all of it. I can only say that I always had the strong desire to combine opposites and let them peacefully co-exist. That's what the instrument does for me. I don't have to do much, just play it. In Africa they say that someone who is playing the harp is connecting the spirits with the physical world. They're not so wrong.

TS: Andreas, did you have any idea that your first LP would be such a big hit?

AV: No, we were really surprised. It was made as an experiment. Finally friends said that we should release it. It wasn't originally planned to be a record. It was a very historic moment in my life. It taught me that if you have too many expectations when you go in the studio, your hope has built up. And with a skyscraper of expectations, you probably will not find what's waiting inside of you to be brought out. I learned that I would like to keep it the same way every time, not to feel I'm under any pressure.

TS: You've sold more than 500,000 copies of each of your albums. Do you enjoy that type of fame? You seem rather shy.

AV: I don't see myself as famous. First of all, I do not live here. Where I live in Switzerland I can deal with it. It's easy. I don't play there so much, and people don't know me so well. And the people who like this kind of music are not the kind of people who roll over me, who want an autograph. Most of them could easily be my friends too. So I do not feel so much of a distance.

TS: Your music has been called "New Age" music. Does that mean anything to you?

AV: To my life it doesn't mean anything. I have made this kind of music all my life. I don't see any "New Age."

TS: Do you think the New Age phenomenon is something that could only happen in America? Europe seems to be much more political an environment.

AV: Yes. I think that the desire to change the society of America is very strong by people who have woken up and seen that something has to be changed. But first we have to clean up the mess we have made. We have to closely study evil before we can create good. We cannot just let evil be in the past, and concentrate on a beautiful, harmonious future. We have to live a conscious life in all its aspects. Evil and greediness must be acknowledged as part of our selves. Maybe that's the reason why this desire to start fresh has a name now, and that name is "New Age." Sounds great, but that's not enough, just to give a name to it. We all have to do it.

TS: Do you think that music can do something to help make the world a better place?

AV: I don't think that it can in itself change something. Music is environment. It's as much environment as your furniture, or the pictures on the wall. We react very strongly to the environment. It is largely responsible for the thoughts which we allow to come out, which will, in turn, modify the environment. We want the environment to give beauty more of a chance, the transparent beauty which is not only to be found in a flower which is fresh coming out of the ground, but can also be found in a dead flower. But we have to search for it.

TS: Does it bother you when you get into an elevator here and you hear your music coming out over the little speaker?

AV: Let me put it this way. Do you have a typewriter?

TS: Yeah.

AV: You can put your typewriter on the top of the roof of your house. Even your car you could put up there. But it's not made for there. So as long as I know this music is not played just in elevators, it's fine. But if I find out it's played only in elevators, I would stop and do something else.

TS: Do you listen to other music?

AV: I try to live a rather silent life. I make it hard for music to reach me, because otherwise it's just stuffing the ears. If I listen to music, it can be from old, different kinds of cultures. I have to feel that its intention is pure.

TS: Are you a religious person?

AV: Yes. This is a large, large question. Religion, in the sense of the word, means "being held back." I think we have to learn how to hold ourselves back without feeling held back, or hindered in our development. There are certain limits. We should see where we end and where we as a collective are continuing. And this also has an end.

TS: You were talking a little bit about good and evil. It seems to me that there is a spiritual element in your music that you've been trying to get across. Do you think that there's some music that's evil, that has a bad effect?

AV: The environment stimulates the being who lives in the environment. If we only live in a negative environment, we tend to be sucked up by the negative. Yet if we try to only live in beauty and keep absolutely away from the negative aspects, we are sucked up by this too, and we are incomplete. We will again create a result which is incomplete.

We have to try to build up within the negative—which is the world which we see—an opposite, to create a friction which will create energy and action. We have to become complete. That's the wonderful plan for us.

1987

TOM WAITS

I TENDED TO ASSOCIATE TOM WAITS' GRAVEL-THROATED SONGS *about life on the skids with Camel straights and cheap whiskey; but when he became a solid family man, there was the same day-after voice. A brilliant writer, a funny admixture of new wave and crooner, Waits can write zany, outrageous songs or simple ballads that cut to the bone.*

One day he dropped in with his own pile of records, joining Janis Siegel of the Manhattan Transfer and myself at the mike.

>*Tom Waits scrounges through a record pile off mike, readying himself to play guest deejay . . .*

TS: Okay, Tom Waits, come on over and just sit down and join us.

TW: I realized it was radio, I was looking for a tie . . .

TS: You don't have to dress up. Just take a look at the people around here . . .

JS: This is very casual . . .

TS: You're living in New York now, right?

TW: I just came in for a couple of weeks and I'm going back to New York in a couple of days. I've been working on a musical

STOLEN MOMENTS

"I have no idea how this really hangs together. It may come off like bad handwriting, I don't know..."

there called *Frank's Wild Years.* It's a story about a disturbing ten years in the life of a very disappointing accordion player who ends up in Las Vegas, despondent and penniless, and East St. Louis.

TS: There's a story about him on *Swordfish Trombones,* your last record.

TW: It's the same Frank, the continuing adventures of Frank O'Brien.

TS: You like New York city life?

TW: It's very angry sometimes. It rears up and chases you all the way home. But I find it culturally stimulating and I like it.

TS: Do you sometimes play guest deejay at home, having friends over and pulling out a million records? At the end of the evening everybody leaves, and you've got a hundred and thirty records on your floor and you've got to put them all away . . .

TW: They usually leave before the end of the evening. (laughs) (*Waits starts to paw through his records again*) I'm not sure where to begin here. This is very schizophrenic. I was up late with some things and I have no idea how this really hangs together. It may come off like bad handwriting, I don't know.

TS: I don't see anything wrong with playing John McCormick [an old-fashioned Irish tenor] next to James Brown.

TW: A lot of people have remarked on that, how they influenced each other. (laughs) Maybe we can keep that in mind as we listen.

(music—tinny, querulous rendition of "God Save Ireland.")

TW: Now we're going to listen to a selection from a Texas Czech Bohemian band's album. These are the early recordings.

TS: As opposed to the middle period, or the be-bop period.

TW: Well the Czech Bohemian people who live in Texas are Slavic people. They came from Bohemia and Moravia, and made a wrong turn. This is about a mutant chemical reaction. It's called "The Circling Pigeons Waltz." It's a sour little number . . .

(music: sour indeed)

TW: Yeah. It's a polka. There's something about the instrumenta-

tion I've always found peculiar, the way it kind of limps along...
TS: What's next?
TW: Well, I have selected a cut of an album of my own. I figure that it's foolish to avoid taking the opportunity to listen to some of my own songs that I enjoy. I don't want to give people the impression that I'm blowing my own horn, but I guess that's exactly what I'm trying to do. This is a song called "Underground." It's on the *Swordfish Trombones* album. It kind of takes you down a rabbit hole.
(Music: Tom Waits' raspy voice . . .)
TW: I'd like to play something by Clifton Chenier next.
TS: You've been a Clifton Chenier fan for a long time?
TW: I have. I'm just learning the accordion, so I have an interest in the instrument, particularly his approach. I've always found it dynamic, unprecedented. He certainly takes it out way beyond the butcher paper and the white socks and puts it in a real brown bag. So let's hear a little something called "Black Snake Blues"...
(music: a raucous zydeco blues)
TS: Tom, you have some Grace Jones lined up?
TW: Yeah. Her and Clifton at least share the same hairdo, so there's a segue in there somewhere...
(music: Grace belts out "Nipple To The Bottle")
TW: In memory of Jack Webb, I thought we'd hear something of *Pete Kelly's Blues*. Then I'd like to go to *James Brown Live at the Apollo*.
TS: It makes perfect sense.
(music)
TW: Let's see. Were are we now?
TS: Igor is waiting on turntable number one.
(Music: Igor Stravinsky's "Tango")
TW plays his record of "16 Shells From a .36." Then he moves into the live recording studio and sits down at the Yamaha Grand. After some trills and moody chords . . .
TW: This is the story of Frank O'Brien who left home and wound up in St. Louis. It was thirty below and he was having a "Going Out of Business Sale" for his life, and he dreamed his

way back home to Rainville where he got his start. So this is called . . . "A Train Can't Bring Me Home."
(A soulful performance of the new song . . .)
TS: We enjoyed that so much, Tom.
JS: Please come back.
TW: Okay.

1985

"I saw Stormy Weather 24 times. It set my life up. That's what I wanted to do."

JOE ZAWINUL

COMPOSER AND PIANIST JOE ZAWINUL'S GRUFF, STREET-HIP *personal manner belies his sophisticated music. But then his story is a unique immigrant saga, taking him from postwar Vienna to New York City, through stints with Cannonball Adderley and Miles Davis. Later he co-founded Weather Report with Wayne Shorter, and wrote the ubiquitous "Birdland." Though a brilliant, classically trained pianist, Zawinul makes no secret of the fact that he prefers state-of-the-art electronics.*

TS: Do you remember, as a young pianist growing up in Vienna, hearing Erroll Garner for the first time?
JZ: Definitely. I tried to copy every note he had played. It developed my left hand a little bit, you know.
TS: One remarkable thing I've heard about is European musicians hearing stuff on Willis Conover's *Voice Of America's Jazz Hour*, before people had cassette decks to tape things, and relying upon their memories to transcribe all that stuff. What a job. And you're one of those people who learned that way.

JZ: Willis Conover played "Honeysuckle Rose." It was the first time I heard jazz, and it changed my life. Then after the war, movies from America started coming in from Austria. Matter of fact, I saw *Stormy Weather* 24 times. It set my life up. That's what I wanted to do.

TS: Was American music easy to hear at the time?

JZ: Americans had radio stations all over Europe. In Vienna we had two or three stations. They played a lot of George Shearing, Benny Goodman, Louis Armstrong. My tendency was more towards the modern sound—Dizzy Gillespie, Miles Davis, Lenny Tristano.

TS: Were you and Friedrich Gulda [Viennese classical pianist] classmates, friends at that time?

JZ: I met Gulda in 1952 in the Art Club in Vienna. We started hanging out almost every night, playing four-hand piano. It was a lot of fun. We listened a lot to Erroll Garner, Bud Powell.

TS: Did you have fantasies about America and what it's like in New York City before you came over?

JZ: Yes, mostly from the films I saw. I wanted to be on this scene, playing with black people, playing the Apollo Theater. And all of these things actually came through. When I was playing with Dinah Washington I was conducting the band in the Apollo Theater, and a lot of the theaters where black acts were performing all over the country. It was a great experience.

TS: You came to the United States from Vienna in 1959, and it didn't take long for things to start happening. Do you remember the day the plane came in?

JZ: Actually it was the boat.

TS: Do you remember the first smell of New York City, or what you first saw?

JZ: I almost had a fight first thing, because the cab driver tried to charge me sixteen dollars from Pier 47 to 52nd Street. It was a very short drive, but he knew I couldn't speak English. And that was a good beginning. You have to stand on your own feet.

TS: Then what happened?

JZ: I went to Birdland the first night, met a few musicians. Next day I went to Berklee School. I had a scholarship. I think I stayed there about two weeks. One evening Ella Fitzgerald was working at Storyville, and the house piano player got sick. They called me up. The next day I auditioned at the Apollo Theater for Maynard Ferguson and got the job. I was in the band for two or three weeks. We needed a tenor player, and Wayne Shorter was one of the guys auditioning. And Wayne got the gig! Then Art Blakey heard Wayne play. Then I got fired.

But a day or two later, Dinah Washington saw me and invited me to come down to the Village Vanguard to opening night. She saw me in the audience and called me up to the bandstand. So that was another little episode. I stayed with her for about 21 months. I got back to New York, and the phone rings and there's a long distance call from Cannonball Adderley.

TS: Your head must have been swimming.

JZ: There were some good times, and learning times. And that's what it was about: Time.

TS: Quite a different type of schooling than you got in the conservatory.

JZ: Well, I'll tell you something. I was never one of the students, in a sense. I was more or less of a street person. I played a lot of sports. I took care of my lessons, but I don't think I was made for classical music. I always enjoyed improvising and rhythm.

TS: It seems you're involved in finding new combinations of sounds, new things you can do with the equipment that you have. Do you ever get sentimental and walk over to the acoustic piano at home?

JZ: I always play the acoustic piano. To me, it's like a boxer would train on a heavy bag. The acoustic piano is for practicing. It's where you get your power. See, today with the technology you can get any sound. You have a hell of a good ear, but you wouldn't be able to tell the difference between an acoustic piano and what I have right now.

TS: Speaking of boxing, I understand you're a fan, and you work out. What's the relationship between boxing and making music?

JZ: Coordination. Judgment of distance. Eye and hand coordination. Eye and leg coordination. Especially what I'm doing—with the synthesizers, foot pedals, etcetera. It works together.

TS: Miles Davis has also always been a boxing fan.

JZ: We used to go to the fights all the time together in New York.

TS: Did Miles influence the way you thought?

JZ: Ever since I heard Miles the first time—it was *The Birth of the Cool*—it knocked me out. It was a big change. I think it's one of the greatest recordings ever. It had a long-lasting hold on me.

TS: Joe, as a young kid did you ever think or dream that you were going to be a member of a big name band touring the world, that you would be playing these advanced instruments, that there would even be music like this?

JZ: It's nothing to brag about, but I used to hear the big bands and I'd say to myself, "If I could play all those instruments it would be a hell of a band." And fortunately now with all the good technology happening, I can do that, and it's wonderful.

1988

A SELECTED DISCOGRAPHY

This list of recordings is not meant to be comprehensive. I simply want to indicate my favorite music by the artists contained in this book. The album title is followed by record label and catalog number.

JOHN ADAMS
   The Chairman Dances (NONESUCH #979144-3)

KING SUNNY ADE
   Synchro System (ISLAND #MLPS 9737)
   Aura (ISLAND #90177)

MOSE ALLISON
   Greatest Hits (FANTASY OJC-6004)

LAURIE ANDERSON
   Mister Heartbreak (WARNER BROS 9-25077-1)

JOAN BAEZ
   Very Early Joan (VANGUARD 9025077-1, VSD 79446/7)

JONATHAN BOROFSKY
   Radical Songbirds of Islam (w/Ed Tomney) (ROIR A-149)

STOLEN MOMENTS

DAVID BYRNE
My Life in the Bush of Ghosts (w/Brian Eno) (SIRE SRK-6093)
The Catherine Wheel (WARNER BROS 9-27418-B)
Music for the Knee Plays (ECM 25022)

JOHNNY CLEGG
Third World Child (EMI/CAPITOL EMC-3526)
Shadow Man (EMI/CAPITOL C1-90411)

LEONARD COHEN
I'm Your Man (COLUMBIA FC 44191)

MICHAEL FEINSTEIN
Isn't it Romantic (ELEKTRA 9-0792-1)

PHILIP GLASS
Glass Works (CBS FM-37 265)
Akhnaten (CBS M2K 42457)
Powaqqatsi (CBS 979192-2)

JOE JACKSON
Big World (A&M SP8021)
Will Power (A&M SP-3908)

KEITH JARRETT
The Köln Concert (ECM 1064)
Spirits (ECM 133314)
Still Live (ECM #1360/1)
Bach/The Well Tempered Clavier (ECM 1362/3)

KIRI TE KANAWA
Canteloube: Songs of the Auvergne (LONDON 410 004-2)
Duparc Seven Songs/Ravel Scheherazade (EMI/ANGEL 7471112)

MIRIAM MAKEBA
Miriam Makeba (RCA LSP 2267)
Sangoma (WARNER BROS 25673)

BRANFORD MARSALIS
Renaissance (CBS 40711)
Random Abstract (CBS OC-44055)

JOHN McLAUGHLIN
Birds of Fire (CBS KC 31996)
My Goal's Beyond (ELEKTRA/MUSICIAN EL-60031)
Belo Horizonte (WARNER BROS BSK 3619)

FRANCIS PAUDRAS
La Danse des Infidels (PARIS, L'INSTANT 1986). A BIOGRAPHY OF BUD POWELL.
To Bird With Love (w/Chan Parker) (POITIERS, EDITIONS WIZLOV, 1981).
A TRIBUTE IN PHOTO AND TEXT TO CHARLIE PARKER.

DISCOGRAPHY

PENGUIN CAFE ORCHESTRA
Penguin Cafe Orchestra (EDITIONS EG EGM 113)
Broadcasting from Home (EDITIONS EG EGED 38)

ASTOR PIAZZOLLA
Tango/Zero Hour (PANGAEA PAND 42138)
Concerto for Bandoneon & Orchestra (NONESUCH 9 79174-2)

STEVE REICH
Sextet/Six Marimbas (NONESUCH 9 79138)
Music for a Large Ensemble/Octet (ECM 1168)

BOBBIE ROBERTSON
Robbie Robertson (GEFFEN GHS 24160)

RYUICHI SAKAMOTO
Neo Geo (CBS BFE 40994)
Illustrated Musical Encyclopedia (MIDI/10 DIX 34)
Futurista (SCHOOL MD 1015)
The Last Emperor (VIRGIN V-2485)
Merry Christmas Mr Lawrence (MCA 6125)

RAVI SHANKAR
Homage to Mahatma Gandhi (DEUTSCHE GRAMMOPHON 2531 356)
Raga Mishra Piloo (w/Ali Akbar Khan) (ANGEL DS 37920)

WAYNE SHORTER
Native Dancer (COLUMBIA PC 33418)
Atlantis (COLUMBIA FC 40055)
Speak No Evil (BLUE NOTE BST 84195)

NINA SIMONE
Nina Simone at Town Hall (REISSUE) (OFFICIAL RECORDS COPENHAGEN 6012)
My Baby Just Cares for Me (CHARLY CD 6)

NICOLAS SLONIMSKY
Perfect Pitch (NEW YORK, OXFORD UNIVERSITY PRESS, 1988). AN AUTOBIOGRAPHY.

MERCEDES SOSA
En Argentine (PHILIPS 6636 051)

RICHARD STOLTZMAN
Begin Sweet World (RCA AMLI 7124)

YMA SUMAC
Legend of the Sun Virgin (CAPITOL SM 299)
Mambo! (CAPITOL 11892)

TANGERINE DREAM
Live in Poland — The Warsaw Concert (JIVE ELECTRO HIP22)

BERTRAND TAVERNIER
Round Midnight—soundtrack (COLUMBIA SC 40464)

STOLEN MOMENTS

ANDREAS VOLLENWEIDER
    Caverna Magica (CBS FM 37827)

TOM WAITS
    Rain Dogs (ISLAND 90299)
    Swordfish Trombones (ISLAND 90095-1)
    Frank's Wild Years (ISLAND 90572)

JOE ZAWINUL
    Zawinul (ATLANTIC SD1579)
    Dialects (CBS FC 40081)

PHOTO CREDITS

Adrian Boot (KING SUNNY ADE); David A. Shanen (MOSE ALLISON); Lynn Goldsmith (LAURIE ANDERSON); Matthew Rolston (JOAN BAEZ); Dennis Keeley (DAVID BYRNE, JOHNNY CLEGG, PHILIP GLASS, STEVE REICH); Sharon Weisz (LEONARD COHEN); Timothy White (MICHAEL FEINSTEIN); Christian Steiner (KIRI TE KANAWA); Susanne Stevens (KEITH JARRETT); William Coupon (MIRIAM MAKEBA); Deborah Feingold (BRANFORD MARSALIS); Francis Paudras (BUD POWELL, FRANCIS PAUDRAS); Stephen Laufer (ASTOR PIAZZOLLA, ROBBIE ROBERTSON, NICOLAS SLONIMSKY); Mark Holmes (RYUICHI SAKAMOTO); Jan Stewart (RAVI SHANKAR); Christopher Landergren (WAYNE SHORTER); John Pearson (RICHARD STOLTZMAN); W.G. Harris (YMA SUMAC); Darryl Pitt (ANDREAS VOLLENWEIDER); Sergio Albonico (JOE ZAWINUL)

Thanks to Steven Baker, Richard Frankel, and Lydia Sarno. And especially to Dennis Keeley.

And a very special thanks to Michael Hodgson and Clive Piercy of P*h*.D for their superb job in designing this book.